backcountry

BEAR BASICS

The Definitive Guide to Avoiding Unpleasant Encounters

D1051804

DAVE SMITH

THE
MOUNTAINEERS

*This book is dedicated to my parents, who let me run wild in the woods
while the other kids were stuck in Sunday school*

———————————

Published by
The Mountaineers
1001 SW Klickitat Way
Seattle, WA 98134

1 0 9 8 7
5 4 3 2 1

Published simultaneously in Canada by Douglas & McIntyre, Ltd., 1615 Venables Street, Vancouver, B.C. V5L 2H1

Published simultaneously in Great Britain by Cordee, 3a DeMontfort Street, Leicester, England, LE1 7HD

Manufactured in the United States of America

Edited by Dana Fos
Illustrations by Mary McEachern
Cover and book design by Ani Rucki
Book layout by Brian Metz

Cover photographs: Main image: © Larry Aumiller, Alaska Dept. of Fish and Game; Inset: *Hiker hanging food in bear country* © Kirkendall/Spring

Library of Congress Cataloging-in-Publication Data
Smith, Dave, 1950–
    Backcountry bear basics : the definitive guide to avoiding unpleasant encounters / Dave Smith.
        p.   cm.
    Includes bibliographical references and index.
    ISBN 0-89886-500-X
    1. Bear attacks—North America—Prevention. 2. Outdoor recreation—North America—Safety measures. 3. Black bear—Behavior. 4. Grizzly bear—Behavior. I. Title.
QL737.C27S6   1997
599.78—dc21   97–4241
                                                        CIP

contents

Acknowledgments / 5
Introduction / 7

Planning a Trip into Bear Country / 11
Bear Evolution, Behavior, and Biology / 15
Menstruation, Sex, and Bears / 29
Cooking and Food Storage / 41
Camping and Travel Tips / 56
Bears and Human Recreation / 72
Close Encounters / 79
Guns and Pepper Spray / 87
Grizzly Bear Recovery and Reintroduction / 93

Notes / 102
Recommended References / 106
Index / 108

acknowledgments

It seems like Doug Peacock and I have spent more time talking about what to cook for dinner than the food habits of bears; nevertheless, his respect for the rights of grizzlies has had an enormous influence on my thoughts about the great bear.

My thanks for reviewing the manuscript go to Larry Aumiller (Alaska Department of Fish and Game), Tom Beck (Colorado Division of Wildlife), Steve French (Yellowstone Grizzly Foundation), Kerry Gunther (Yellowstone National Park), Polly Hessing, Colleen Matt (Alaska Department of Fish and Game), Rick McAdam (Yellowstone National Park), Lewis Sharman (Glacier Bay National Park), and Derek Stonorov (Alaska Department of Fish and Game). I'm also grateful to Mike Swain and Ed Vorisek (Denali National Park) and Lisa Peacock for reviewing portions of the manuscript.

In phone conversations and correspondence, Steve French and Tom Beck were generous with their time and their understanding of bears. There's no way I can express my gratitude to the McNeil River crew—Larry Aumiller, Polly Hessing, Colleen Matt, and Derek Stonorov—for sharing their knowledge of bears with me. Colleen in particular helped shape the book with her gentle insistence on finding ways to reach people with accurate facts about bears.

Others who helped along the way include Larry Campbell (Friends of the Bitterroot), Jasper Carlton (Biodiversity Legal Foundation), Mitch Friedman (Greater Ecosystem Alliance), Keith Hammer (Swan View Coalition), Ken Leghorn (Alaska Discovery), Lynn Rogers, Roger Rudolph, John Scheerens, Tom Walker, and Louisa Willcox (Wild Forever).

If I've left anyone out, my apologies. If there are any factual errors in this book, they're mine and mine alone.

Opposite: *During most so-called "maulings," bears exercise considerable restraint, just as they do when playing with each other.* (Larry Aumiller)

introduction

The bears of remote areas, unaccustomed to human traffic, may
be more timid than average.
> —*John Hart*, Walking Softly in the Wilderness:
> The Sierra Club Guide to Backpacking, *1983*

It is mainly wild black bears found in rural or remote areas—
where they have relatively little association with people—that
occasionally try to kill and eat a human being.
> —*Stephen Herrero*,
> Bear Attacks: Their Causes and Avoidance, *1985*

Bear literature is confusing and contradictory. Inaccurate assumptions masquerade as biological axioms, and conventional wisdom about bears is often just bad advice. The same books and brochures that advise you to climb a tree to safety to escape a charging grizzly insist that you should never run from a bear. They tell you not to run because flight can trigger pursuit and you won't win a race with a bear; they say climb a tree instead, because adult grizzlies can't. Whoa. Hold on. Before you start climbing, ask yourself two critical questions. First, if flight is likely to trigger pursuit, won't grizzlies chase tree-climbers and track stars with equal abandon? Second, how much time will you have to squirrel up a tree when you startle a grizzly at 60 yards or less? Conventional wisdom may say climb a tree to safety, but knowing that a bear can outrun you tells you that sprinting for and then trying to climb a tree after a bear begins its charge is a dangerous mistake—you won't have time.

What about the widespread belief that bears have poor vision? Is it true, or is it a myth based on the tall tales of mountain men? This is not an academic question when you spot a female grizzly with two cubs 80 yards away. Let's say the bears are not aware of your presence. A steady 12-mile-per-hour wind is blowing in your face. The bears aren't going to smell you, and they won't hear you if you keep quiet. So can they see you standing there? Will they spot you if you move? You need to know because their visual acuity dictates your next move.

Backcountry Bear Basics will separate facts from fallacies and give you detailed information on how to travel and camp safely in bear country. The emphasis will be on preventing unpleasant incidents; first choose a good campsite and properly store your food, and then worry about whether or not pepper spray will protect you from a bear investigating your camp.

I try to allow the natural behavior and habits of bears to guide my conduct when I'm afield. Statistics prove that hiking with four or more people significantly reduces the likelihood of a bear attack, largely because more people tend to make more noise—you're less likely to startle a bear at close range. I prefer the risks (and rewards) of traveling alone to the guilt I feel for hiking with a noisy mob of people that displaces bears from their preferred habitat. Although I clap my hands or call out loudly when I'm in thick cover, I don't go to extremes like blasting portable boat horns. We can't ignore the fact that even nonlethal methods of enhancing human safety in bear country can be detrimental to bears, especially our beleaguered grizzlies in the Lower 48 states. In *Backcountry Bear Basics,* I'll explain your options, describe the consequences of your actions on bears, and let your conscience be your guide.

Hikers and hunters agree that bears are exceptionally intelligent creatures, yet the February 1995 cover of *Backpacker* magazine featured an article titled "The Real Truth about Grizzlies: Why You Have Little to Fear," while that same month the cover of *Outdoor Life* magazine had a piece titled "Should We Hunt Grizzlies: A Tale of Terror Holds the Answer." Why would an intelligent animal flee from unarmed hikers yet charge hunters toting a .375 H&H Magnum rifle capable of dropping an elephant? This suicidal behavior suggests that either bears are stupid or people twist facts to make bears into whatever we want them to be. Bears aren't stupid. Nor are grizzly bears territorial, but it's a lot easier to say "grizzlies attack humans to defend their territory" than it is to look for the real reasons why bears injure people. From the modern myth that menstruating women should stay out of bear country to the old misconception that bears have difficulty running downhill, bear literature is rife with erroneous information and self-serving facts.

Pejorative language limits our knowledge of bears. In *Yosemite: The Embattled Wilderness,* historian Alfred Runte notes that even well-meaning bear advocates use terms like "marauding," "offending," and "troublesome" to describe the very bears they're dedicated to protecting.[1] You won't encounter any "problem bears" in *Backcountry Bear Basics,* and we're going to examine the veracity of clichés about "unpredictable bears" making "bluff charges." Clichés and pejorative language act as blinders that keep you from seeing bears for what they really are; they prevent you from understanding what bears are all about.

Sound information about bears is vital because what you don't know about bears can endanger you. Consider the following excerpt from an article in *Field & Stream,* which was accompanied by a picture of a bear down on all fours directly facing the photographer who wrote the story:

> Every few minutes, the sow grizzly raised her head and stared at me. Satisfied that I posed no threat, she continued to devour red soap berries from the brushy Alaskan slope. The sow probably weighed 350 pounds, but at 70 feet, she appeared much larger. . . . I watched intently for any indication that she was unhappy with my presence in her territory, but there was none. The hair on her neck was not raised in alarm, and she made no noise other than the guttural sounds that come from a bear gathering a berry breakfast. . . . Suddenly, without warning, she charged![2]

I'm not sure what sort of warning the author expected—maybe he thought the bear was going to pick up a megaphone and say, "Back off chump," but any wild animal that frequently stops feeding or other activities to watch you is a bit uneasy. Whether you're watching bears or porcupines, you have an ethical obligation to stop bothering the animal, and it's just plain stupid to keep pressing a grizzly bear that's only 70 feet away. During an encounter between two bears, frontal orientation—facing directly toward an antagonist—can signify dominance or a willingness to attack. In other words, the bear in our story expressed its anxiety with a person who was way too close, but the photographer didn't recognize the signs. Ignorance is not bliss in bear country, and if you go afield with preconceptions about bears that are misconceptions, your false assumptions could prove costly.

Brown bears in the Pyrenees Mountains of Spain are the same species as North America's fabled grizzlies, yet centuries of human domination and selective killing that eliminates the boldest bears have turned them into ghosts that are rarely seen. Illegal hunting, incremental habitat loss, and incessant harassment by everyone from mountain bikers to bubbleheads on snowmobiles might turn Yellowstone's grizzlies into ghost bears. They may adapt and survive, but their haunting presence would only serve as a reminder of all that's been lost. Instead of *Ursus arctos horriblis,* we'll have *Ursus arctos emasculatis.* I refuse to accept that, so my goal for writing *Backcountry Bear Basics* goes beyond giving tips to make your trip to bear country safer; I want to make the world a better place for bears. Fortunately, these two objectives go hand in hand. I'm convinced that if we can accommodate bears in our world, it will be a better place for us to live, too.

Planning a Trip into Bear Country

As with most safety issues, proper preparation for bear country camping begins before the trip.
—*Ken Leghorn*, Sea Kayaker *magazine, 1987*

Planning for a trip into bear country involves learning a bit about bears and the area you intend to visit, packing essential equipment, and making sure you have the proper attitude—you accept the risks of traveling in bear country and accept responsibility for the consequences of your actions.

RESEARCH

Always get general information on bear activity in the area you plan to visit well in advance of your trip, and then get up-to-date facts when you arrive. Many parks and forests closely monitor bear activity, and they will be happy to pass on information.

If you're planning months in advance for a trip to Kluane National Park in the Yukon, call or write for basic information and check on the feasibility of your plans. Sometimes people study topographic maps and trail guides and make up their mind they're going to hike to Eagle Peak the first week of September no matter what. When they arrive in Kluane, they discover the Eagle Peak area is closed because several grizzly bears have gathered there to feast on huckleberries. There's a temptation to hike in anyhow. So what if it's dangerous? Who cares if you drive away a few bears? You've been thinking about this trip for six months.

If you had called in advance, somebody could have told you the Eagle Peak area has been closed in September for the past three years. Resource management experts can often predict when and where to expect bears because the bruins are so keyed in to seasonal food sources. You might save yourself from disappointment or disaster by contacting land managers well in advance of your trip and asking for their recommendations.

Once you arrive at your destination, even if you're not required to check in and get a permit before setting off on a hike or canoe trip, it's still a good idea to get up-to-date information on the places you plan to visit. You don't want to camp at a site that a bear raided the night before. Also, check the signs at trailheads for up-to-the-minute notices.

Part of your advance planning should include researching bears themselves and how they interact with humans. There are several good books and videos available about bears (see "Recommended References"), and once you've checked a few sources you'll be well prepared for an excursion into bear country. Just as importantly, you will have less fear of bears, which is often just a fear of the unknown.

What if there's a black bear in your camp at night? What if a grizzly bear charges you? It's important to know how you should—or shouldn't—respond to bears during close encounters. You have to focus on bears before you go afield, not after you've hiked 2 miles. People have been killed by bears "just a half-mile from the trailhead." Don't make the mistake of thinking the bears are "out there" and you're safe near human artifacts on the edge of wildlands. Be knowledgeable and alert the instant you enter the woods.

During a close-up with a bear, yawning is a sign of low-level stress. (Larry Aumiller)

BEAR ESSENTIALS

Don't forget special bear paraphernalia as you pack for your trip. If you're the type of person who uses a camping equipment checklist, put the "bear gear" you plan on using at the top of the list:

- ✔ A bear-resistant food container (see the chapter, "Cooking and Food Storage")
- ✔ Resealable plastic bags and garbage bags ("Cooking and Food Storage")
- ✔ Fifty to 100 feet of cord or rope and two stuff sacks for hanging food, if you use the counterbalance method ("Cooking and Food Storage")
- ✔ Binoculars ("Camping and Travel Tips")
- ✔ A tent ("Camping and Travel Tips")
- ✔ A flashlight ("Camping and Travel Tips")
- ✔ Pepper spray ("Guns and Pepper Spray")
- ✔ A sheath knife with a 3- to 5-inch blade or a folding knife with a locking blade ("Close Encounters")

Some people tote firearms in places where it's legal, but you should carefully consider the information in "Guns and Pepper Spray" before packing a firearm.

PRECAUTIONS WITH CHILDREN

Discuss bears with your kids before you go. A recent statistical report on fatal injuries inflicted by black bears presented at the Fifth Western Black Bear Workshop shows that out of thirty-seven documented cases of black bears killing people, five cases involved children ten years and under and another five cases involved people between the ages of ten and nineteen.[3] I don't think we can say black bears target children as prey because of their small size; however, I do believe it's prudent to try to make your kids understand that bears can be dangerous. Have a talk with your children before going afield, but keep it simple:

1. Never let the adult(s) you're with out of sight.
2. Don't approach bears or other wildlife.
3. Never run from a bear.
4. If you see a bear, don't scream.
5. Stay calm and call loudly for help when you see a bear.

Remember, though, that despite your forceful little speech kids always seem to wander off and disappear. It's up to you to keep close tabs on your children. When hiking, always keep kids between adults, not at the front or rear of your group.

RESPONSIBILITY

One final note of caution about bear country: The government is not responsible for your safety in bear country—you are. As a general rule, you can get accurate information from rangers and agency personnel about such things as high- and low-density bear areas and locations where bears have been seen recently, but agency folks cannot guarantee your safety in bear country. Just because there weren't any bears on the Whitebark Pine Trail for the past three weeks does not mean you won't bump into one today. All the agencies can do is give you their best educated guess about a complex situation that any bear can change anytime it wants. Again—there's no guarantee of your safety in bear country. If you're injured by a bear, don't blame anyone but yourself. If you're not willing to accept responsibility for your decision to go afield in bear country, go somewhere else.

Bear Evolution, Behavior, and Biology

Beyond a general knowledge of bear biology, such as the physical differences between grizzlies and black bears, it's helpful to know a little about the evolution of bears to understand why they behave the way they do, and it's wise to be familiar with the basics of bear behavior so you don't think a nearby bear that yawns at you is bored when in fact it's a bit stressed. Understanding how bears interact with other bears is the key to understanding how bears interact with humans and, in turn, to making the correct moves when you have a close encounter with a bear. This chapter will emphasize the aspects of bear biology, behavior, and evolution that count for backcountry users.

EVOLUTION

> Bears are wild animals that demand your respect. Strong and
> agile, they will defend themselves, their young, and their territory
> if they feel threatened.
>
> —*Environment Canada Parks Service,*
> You Are in Bear Country, *1990*

Because black bears and grizzly bears walked along different evolutionary paths, the two species often have a different response to what biologists call the "fight or flight" question: How do you respond to a threatening situation? Do you fight, or do you take flight?

Black bears are creatures of the forest, so in response to a threat they've always had the option of slipping into the underbrush and hiding or climbing a tree. When threatened, black bears flee. Even when black bear biologists hold squalling cubs while mama bear is just yards away, the females almost always retreat. They may make a blowing sound and clack their teeth and make a rush or two toward the biologists but, ultimately, they retreat.

Not so with grizzlies. Grizzlies evolved in more open terrain. At times, there wasn't enough cover for a female and her cubs to hide from other bears or mammals. There were no trees to climb. When threatened, a female had to defend her cubs.

The key word here is *defend*. Grizzlies aren't malicious beasts that lurk in the woods waiting to waylay backpackers. A grizzly may defend itself if it perceives you as a threat but, if you don't bother a grizzly, it will rarely bother you. I realize that's no comfort to a person who accidentally startles a grizzly at close range and gets injured. I'm not pretending that grizzlies are harmless teddy bears. I just want to make it clear that, in evolutionary terms, it's perfectly natural for grizzlies to defend themselves and their cubs. There's no right or wrong in this, no good or bad. It's an instinctive reaction based on thousands of years of evolutionary history.

One of the most common explanations for bear attacks is that the bear was "defending its territory." Bears are not territorial. A territorial animal excludes others of its own kind from a specific area. Bears have home ranges that overlap.

When people say bears are territorial, they probably mean that a bear might take offense if you encroach into the immediate area around it. Just as people have a personal space, bears (and all other animal species) have a comfort zone around them. Ethologists call this area an animal's *individual distance*. The textbook definition of individual distance is "that distance that if entered will cause the animal to attack or flee." Biologist Polly Hessing uses the term *magic circle* to describe a bear's individual distance.[4] Once you're "engaged" in a bear's magic circle, it will feel compelled to do "something." It might come closer to identify you or better assess the situation, but, ultimately, you've forced it into a situation where it can only flee or attack.

The magic circle around every bear is different and constantly changes in size and shape. As an example, the magic circle of a female grizzly with spring cubs will probably be larger than the magic circle of the same bear when she doesn't have cubs. There are a multitude of factors that determine the size of a bear's magic circle at a given moment, and because you're not likely to know what they are, it's best to keep your distance. The more distance you keep between yourself and bears, the less the chance you'll step inside their magic circle.

Don't forget that you have a magic circle, too. A seasoned black bear biologist might be comfortable with a bear that's only 10 yards away, but you or I might be nervous about a black bear that's 40 yards away. If you want to be safe in bear country and minimize your effects on the animals, distance is the key. Keep your distance.

Defensive aggression, a female defending her cubs, is an entirely different type of behavior than predatory aggression. The difference is immediately apparent when you compare the body language of a grizzly bear digging an Arctic ground squirrel out of its den to the body language of a female grizzly with two cubs facing down a dominant male bear at a crowded fishing hole. At the very least, you'll notice that the female defending her cubs lowers her head and lays her ears back. Anybody with a cat or dog has seen similar body language. Now think of your pet's body language when it's chasing a ball or a piece of yarn: ears up, eyes wide open, intensely alert, yet somehow relaxed. Compare that to the way your pet looks when it's angry or frightened or involved in a tense, close-up situation with another cat or dog.

When an animal clicks into a predatory mode, the anger and stress you see during defensive aggression is absent. A black bear hunting moose calves is about as angry at the moose calf as a butcher is at the chickens he or she is chopping apart. When a black bear kills and eats a person, we usually say the bear is "too aggressive" and kill it. The fact is, a black bear that preys on humans is no more aggressive than a black bear that preys on moose calves or ants; it's just hunting a different animal. The issue isn't aggression, it's the bear's choice of prey.

Given that humans are plentiful, slow afoot, relatively small, and weak for our size, it's surprising that bears don't prey on people more often. It would certainly be easier for a grizzly to catch a hiker with bad blisters on his feet than a caribou with a twisted knee. The rarity of bear predation on humans tells me we don't often fit their prey image like marmots, mice, and salmon do. Still, I'm not willing to dismiss predation as an unnatural act or the desperate deed of a starving or slightly crazed individual. Our culture can deem bear predation on humans as socially unacceptable; however, in terms of pure biology, predation on humans is well within the bounds of natural behavior for bears. Our inability to accept these rare deaths is curious when compared to the attitude Africans have toward crocodiles or to the acceptance by people in India and Bangladesh of man-eating tigers, which kill hundreds of people a year.

BEHAVIOR

As more and more people crowd into bear country, the same intelligence and curiosity that helped black and grizzly bears survive through the ages often lead to conflicts with humans. While such conflicts are often attributed to the "unpredictable" nature of bears most problems result from a failure on our part to store food securely or handle garbage properly, resulting in food-conditioned bears. This brings bears close to people, and people are generally intolerant of bears.

Animal trainers like Doug Suess, who works with TV and movie star Bart the Kodiak bear, point out that you only have to show bears how to do something one time, maybe twice, and they've got it.[5] In Yosemite, that kind of intelligence has given us bears who specialize at breaking into a particular make, model, and year of car. Once a bear figures out how to rip open the door on a 1987 Toyota Corolla, you're out of luck if you park yours at a trailhead. For backcountry users, bear intelligence means that if a bear happens to find food in a pack at your campsite it's likely to return again and again to look for food in the packs of other campers. One mistake and you train the bear to bother other campers.

Curious bears often make a slow, halting approach toward people, other bears, and intriguing objects. They crane their neck, their ears are cocked forward, their head and nose are up, and they sniff, sniff, sniff. They might huff, too.

In Denali, where food-conditioned bears are a rarity, most property damage stems from bears just checking things out—your tent, for example. While you're gone on a day hike, a grizzly will come along and give a tentative push on your tent with its paw. It's easy to imagine the bear's thoughts at this point: "Wow. It springs right back. This is fun. I wonder what would happen if I bit this thing?" It doesn't take much effort for a grizzly to bite a free-standing tent, pick it up, shake it, and just have a good ol' time. Bears in Denali destroy several tents every summer in this manner. They're just curious.

One of bear expert Doug Peacock's favorite stories involves a bear that made its way into a Park Service patrol cabin in Glacier National Park. It bit into cans of ham and baked beans and almost all the other goodies it found—but not the cans of sauerkraut.

For some reason, bears are interested in petroleum products. When they come across a spot of oil or gas on the ground, they sometimes roll in it like a dog rolls on a carcass. After the Exxon Valdez oil spill, some bears looked like they'd been using Brylcream. My friend Hod Coburn, a bush pilot who's flown all over Alaska, told me that a black bear once got into a case of oil he stashed at a remote runway in the western part of the state. It didn't bite one can and assume there was more of the same in the others— it bit into every can. Several biologists have reported that bears have bitten campers' fuel bottles; if you take a stove and fuel bottle on your outdoor excursions, play it safe and store them with your food and garbage.

I wouldn't go so far as to say bears have a rubber fetish, but they do have a thing about rubber rafts, polyethylene kayaks, foam sleeping pads, and buoys from crab pots. If an object has any spring or bounce, a bear is likely to play with it. This includes plastic and Styrofoam ice chests because they give a little before they break. It doesn't matter whether you have a brand new ice chest or one that reeks of fish; they're all fun for bears. Plastic water bottles are fair game, too.

Anyone who's done much kayaking along the coast of Southeast Alaska or British Columbia knows that you can do everything right—cook below the high tide line, store your food and odorous items in a bear can, and pitch your tent 100 yards upwind from your food storage area—and when you wake up in the morning, tracks in the mud and sand will tell you that a bear walking along the beach at night noticed your tent, made a detour for it, checked things out, and then went back the way it came.

One year the biologists at Alaska's McNeil River cut and stacked a few driftwood logs on a beach in front of their quarters. Bears had been walking by the uncut and scattered logs all summer, but now they had something new in their environment. They scattered the firewood. They couldn't stay away from it. There's nothing malicious about the curiosity of bears. It evolved as a food-finding strategy. It's perfectly natural behavior. Bears are so curious they'll try almost anything once—except sauerkraut.

Bears are curious and will investigate almost anything new in their world. They often sniff, paw, and then bite new objects. (Larry Aumiller)

Bears are commonly described as "unpredictable." Whenever I read that bears are unpredictable, I envision a couple of rednecks traveling to China and watching their first Chinese wedding. With grace and fluidity, the wedding couple moves through the intricate and carefully choreographed steps of a ceremony that's centuries old. Our rednecks make a video of the wedding. When they show the video to friends back home, the audience laughs and howls. "Look at them little Chinese people," shout the hosts. "Ya never know what they's gonna do next."

Right. Them little Chinese people is as unpredictable as bears. We'd ridicule a person who watched his or her first Chinese wedding and then described the proceedings as a series of unpredictable movements by the bride and groom. So shouldn't we question people who say grizzlies are unpredictable? Most people simply don't know enough about bear behavior in general, let alone the personalities of individual bears, to predict what a bear is going to do next. That doesn't mean bears are unpredictable—it means the observer is ignorant. Labeling bears as unpredictable just shuts the door to knowledge and understanding.

So many people have said that bears are unpredictable that novice outdoors people now believe they're at the whim of chance in bear country. Why store food properly? Why worry about the odors of cooking food? No matter what you do, a bear could put you in the hospital. It's just fate. When you believe bears are unpredictable, it's easy to get a "what difference does it make" attitude, and that's dangerous. Bears are predictable. Your actions do count.

Some (but not all) bears quickly "habituate" to humans. They learn to ignore a recurring stimulus like hikers on a trail if there's no reward or punishment involved. When bears aren't punished for associating with people but are rewarded with food, they become food-conditioned. Sometimes food-conditioned bears approach people or campsites in the same manner as curious bears, but they can also be quite bold. They know what they want—your food—and they can be pushy. Black bears will actually make threat displays toward people blocking their way to food.

When you look at photos or film footage of a congregation of bears fishing for salmon at a place like McNeil River or Brooks River in Katmai National Park, you'll often see two bears fighting or two bears just inches apart jawing at each other in a tense situation. When you visit those places yourself, what you see is that smaller bears usually get out of the way of bigger bears and that's that. Even between bears of equal size, serious fights are

When bears are stressed, they froth at the mouth and salivate. (Larry Aumiller)

the exception to the rule. It's almost as though each bear is charged like the positive end of a magnet; whenever two bears get close to each other, they don't touch because the magnetic field keeps them a safe distance apart.

When bears do get close enough for a confrontation, they exhibit signs of stress and use vocalizations and body language to communicate with each other. This prevents fights that could cause serious injuries or death. Yawning and slobbering—a bit of foam on the lips—indicates low-level stress.

If you quickly inhale and instantly blow out so hard your cheeks puff out, you'll imitate the "blowing" sound that black bears commonly make. With grizzly bears it comes out as a "woof." Blowing or woofing may be accompanied by clacking teeth. One bear might blow and make a short lunge toward another bear while slapping its paws on the ground or a tree. Although bears growl and roar during fights, they don't growl to threaten each other or people.

When a young male grizzly gets too close to a mature female with cubs, she might regard him as a threat to her offspring and charge him. He's going to meet her charge with his head down, mouth open, ears back, and his hindquarters lowered in a slight crouch. He signals that he's unwilling to attack yet ready to defend himself. She probably won't make contact because she doesn't want to start what could be a fatal fight.

After introductions, they stand there and make open mouth threats at each other. He can't make any sudden moves or attempt to back away. He can't break off the encounter because she's the dominant bear and he's the subordinate. If he shows any signs of submission, she might pounce on him. He has to meet her first threat with a threat of his own, and even after the initial tension dissipates he's in a delicate position. He can't retreat, he doesn't want to threaten her so much he provokes an attack, yet he must somehow convey that he's ready and willing to defend himself. He does that just by standing there, by not retreating. Standing still signals an unwillingness to attack. He'll probably lower his head very slowly and look at the ground while watching her out of the corner of his eye. She knows he won't attack her, so she can look and move around. Eventually, she'll leave.

Although female bears with cubs will charge large, dominant males, the bear that approaches another bear is usually in control of the situation. During an encounter, bears huff, pant, sniff, walk with their front legs stiffened, lay their ears back, pop their jaws, circle each other, vocalize, and exhibit all sorts of other behaviors. When Alaska Department of Fish and Game biologist Derek Stonorov studied brown bear behavior at McNeil River in the early 1970s for his master's thesis, he found that they routinely used at least forty visual signals to communicate.[6]

There are three key behaviors you need to be aware of:

1. The bear that approaches is usually in command of the situation.
2. The subordinate bear does not end an engagement with a dominant bear; the dominant bear is the first to leave.
3. Merely standing still has signal value: standing still will often alter the ongoing behavior of an approaching bear.

Based on the dynamics of bear–bear encounters, I stand my ground when approached by a bear during a sudden, close-up encounter. I also stand my ground when approached by curious or food-conditioned bears. I'll even clap my hands or act more aggressively toward curious or food-conditioned bears if they persist in coming closer. Such techniques, however, warrant more detail and are discussed in a later chapter, "Close Encounters."

BASIC BIOLOGY

Although dozens of books provide in-depth coverage of bear biology, I'm going to shift the normal focus a little to meet the needs of active outdoors people. The fact that a bear's heartbeat drops by around 80 percent during hibernation is irrelevant to cross-country skiers; however, the fact that a few grizzlies in Yellowstone emerge from their dens in March does have significance for folks on skinny skis—you could bump into a bear at the end of a long, downhill run.

BEAR SPECIES

Black bears (*Ursus americanus*) and brown bears (*Ursus arctos*) are different species. Kodiak bears (*Ursus arctos middendorffi*) have not been genetically isolated on Alaska's Kodiak Island for long enough to be considered a subspecies of the brown bear. They have the same genetic makeup as brown bears along Alaska's coast.[7] Taxonomists list brown bears and grizzly bears as the same species. People generally call *Ursus arctos* along the coast of Alaska "brown bears" and *Ursus arctos* everywhere else "grizzly bears," a convention I follow throughout this book.

Even bear experts can have trouble distinguishing black bears from grizzlies in the field because the key physical differences listed below are not always readily apparent.

GRIZZLY BEAR	BLACK BEAR
Dished/concave facial profile from tip of nose to top of forehead.	Straight line (Roman) facial profile from tip of nose to forehead.
Relatively small, short, rounded ears.	Larger, more erect, pointed ears, especially on cubs and immature bears.
In spring and fall, mature animals may have ruff of hair under chin.	No ruff of hair under chin.
Hump over front shoulder.	No hump over shoulder—but some body postures give appearance of hump.
Shoulder hump is highest point on body.	Back is highest point on body.
Front claws usually at least 1¾ inches long, fairly straight, and light-colored.	Front claws rarely exceed 1½ inches, dark-colored, and often sharply curved for climbing.
Track of hindfoot has pointed heel.	Track of hindfoot has rounded heel.
No wedge in instep of hindfoot.	Wedge in instep of hindfoot.
Straight line drawn across top of main pad on front foot track won't cross toepads.	Straight line drawn across top of main pad of front foot will cross smaller toepads.
Adults often have grizzled (gray-tipped) cape of long hair over shoulders.	Not grizzled, although they can appear to have a grizzled coat in certain lighting conditions.

GRIZZLY BEAR

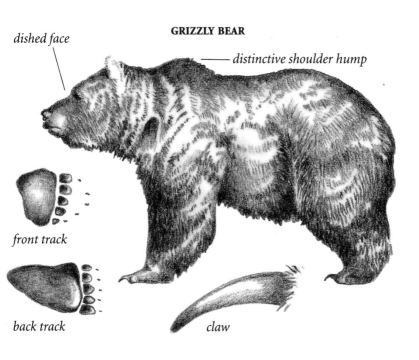

dished face

distinctive shoulder hump

front track

back track

claw

BLACK BEAR

front track

back track

claw

MALE OR FEMALE?

A female's urine stream jets backward from beneath her tail. Males urinate downward from their penile sheath, which is between their hind legs.

SIZE

An average-size mature female black bear in the Brooks Range of Alaska stands 24 to 30 inches tall at the shoulder, measures about 5 feet long from nose to tail, and weighs 120 to 140 pounds. Males average 200 to 300 pounds. In the same area, female grizzlies weigh 220 to 230 pounds, while males weigh 375 to 450 pounds.

In the Rockies, adult male grizzlies weigh 350 to 400 pounds in the spring; females average about 250 pounds. The bears gain 50 to 100 pounds by the time they den in the fall. An adult male will be 6 to 7 feet long and 30 to 36 inches high at the shoulder.

In midsummer, a mature, average-size male Kodiak bear is 7½ feet long, stands 4 feet high at the shoulder, and weighs 850 pounds. A female is 6½ feet long, stands 3½ feet tall at the shoulder, and weighs 450 pounds.

SPEED

Black bears can run 25 to 30 miles per hour and grizzlies are even faster—35 miles per hour is a commonly used figure and some published accounts say 41 miles per hour. By comparison, a fast high-school halfback runs a 40-yard dash in 4.5 seconds—that's 18.2 miles per hour. When you break down these figures into feet per second, the futility of trying to outrun a bear or climb a tree to safety to escape a charging bear is apparent. At 30 miles per hour, a bear covers 44 feet per second. If you're as fast as a high-school halfback, you're covering 26.67 feet per second. Let's say that after startling a bear that's 100 feet away you panic and run. The bear gives chase. It's gaining 17 feet per second on you. In about 6 seconds, it will have you.

What about tree-climbing? You startle a bear that's 100 feet away and decide to run and climb a tree that's only 10 feet away. The bear will arrive in about 3 seconds. You wouldn't have time to climb a stepladder, let alone a tree. Even full-grown black bears can scoot up *any* tree with astonishing speed. An adult grizzly can "ladder" its way up a tree if the limbs are right, with a known record of 33 feet high.

SENSES

Vision: A 1937 report from Europe noted that brown bears in a zoo could see people at 120 yards and recognize their handler at 60 yards.[8]

Although bear vision has not been tested, anecdotal evidence indicates that bears have good vision. Here's an account by Lyle Willmarth, a research technician with the Colorado Division of Wildlife black bear studies:

> I was hunting mule deer near timberline on the upper end of an old logged area. I was dressed in camouflage clothing with a blaze orange vest and hat. I spotted a medium sized black bear crossing the logged area at a distance of 800 yards. I immediately sat down to observe the bear with binoculars. The bear apparently had seen me and he calmly walked to a small clump of trees, which he stopped behind. He held tight for several minutes as I watched. Finally he stuck his head through the limbs and looked directly at me. Within a few minutes he slowly moved off towards the ridgeline, always keeping good cover between himself and me.[9]

Steve French, an M.D. and bear researcher who's co-director of the Yellowstone Grizzly Foundation, has an excellent rule of thumb regarding the vision of bears: If you can see a bear, you should assume that it can see you.

Hearing: Like bear vision, bear hearing has not been tested. Anecdotal evidence suggests that under optimal conditions bears can detect normal human conversation at distances of 300 yards or more.

Smell: Bears have a legendary sense of smell. Bears will stand up on their hind legs to smell and see better. Occasionally, they drop to all fours and circle downwind to confirm things.

HIBERNATION

There are some years when a few bears on Kodiak Island never hibernate. A thousand miles to the north, grizzly bears in the Brooks Range hibernate for six months of the year or more. Some black bears in the South never hibernate, while black bears in Minnesota may spend seven months in their winter den. No matter where you go in bear country, you need to know how late in the fall the bears might remain active and how early they emerge from their dens in the late winter/early spring.

REPRODUCTION

Bears mate in the spring/early summer, and the female gives birth in the den during midwinter. Both black bear and brown bear cubs weigh less than a pound at birth. Litter size ranges from one to six and is typically two or three. Black bears generally stay with their mother for seventeen months.

Grizzly cubs usually stay with their mother for 2½ years, or sometimes even 3½ years. Grizzlies have a low reproductive capacity because females don't breed until the age of five to eight years, and then they care for their cubs for two to three years.

FOOD

Both black and grizzly bears are omnivores, but that doesn't mean they'll eat anything. They eat from a large variety of diverse food groups; however, they may only eat 10 to 25 percent of all the plants species available at a given location. Each plant is generally consumed at a particular time of year—for instance, black bears in Southeast Alaska eat rye grass along the beach in the spring but feast on blueberries in the spruce forest during the fall.

Menstruation, Sex, and Bears

It is well known that odors attract bears. But is there any proof that the odors of menstruation or sex are more attractive to bears than the odors of smelly socks or the sweat-soaked shoulder straps of your pack?

MENSTRUATION

Odors attract bears. . . . Women should stay out of bear country during their menstrual period.
> —*National Park Service/U.S. Forest Service,*
> Grizzly Grizzly Grizzly Grizzly, *1982*

Women should be extra careful. Bears may be attracted to women during their menstrual period.
> —*Glacier National Park/Flathead National Forest,*
> You Are in Grizzly Country, *1995*

A menstruating woman does not smell like a used tampon.
> —*Caroline P. Byrd, "Of Bears and Women: Investigating the*
> *Hypothesis That Menstruation Attracts Bears," 1988*

Ever since Glacier National Park's infamous "night of the grizzlies" in 1967, menacing warnings that *imply* menstrual odors attract bears have needlessly worried women or kept them out of bear country altogether. They've created a fear far out of proportion to the risk. In 1992, however, the Interagency Grizzly Bear Committee (IGBC) began distributing a brochure titled *Women in Bear Country* that states, "There is no evidence that grizzlies are overly attracted to menstrual odors more than they are any other odor and there is no statistical evidence that known attacks have been related to menstruation."

If there's "no evidence that grizzlies are overly attracted to menstrual odors," then why did the National Park Service (NPS) and the Forest Service include menstrual warnings in their bear literature as recently as 1995? Why does the Flathead National Forest still distribute a brochure that says, "Menstruating women should stay out of bear country." Why did the IGBC distribute a brochure in 1985 that said, "Odors and food attract bears. . . . [M]enstruating women may choose to stay out of bear country."[10] That's like posting billboards beside every highway entering Kansas that say, "WARNING—There's no evidence menstruating women are at greater risk than anyone else in tornado country; however, menstruating women should stay out of Kansas during tornado season."

I'm pleased the IGBC is finally trying to set the record straight, but it's probably too late. The menstrual myth is too well established. While there are usually a multitude of possible explanations for a bear attack and many contributing factors, I suspect that ten, twenty, even fifty years from now, if a bear attacks a woman, some people will say, "I'll bet she was menstruating."

Because government brochures have often relied on innuendo and insinuation to convey information about bears and menstruation, discussions of this delicate topic tend to be long on rumors and short on facts. Let's go back to the night of the grizzlies and get all the facts so that women can make an informed decision on whether or not to travel in bear country while menstruating.

NIGHT OF THE GRIZZLIES

On August 13, 1967, two women were killed by grizzly bears in separate incidents in two different backcountry areas of Glacier National Park. Because these were Glacier Park's first bear-related deaths, they attracted intense media coverage and immense public interest. It was a strange and disturbing coincidence that both deaths occurred on the same night and involved young women. "The mystery," said an article in *Sports Illustrated,* "triggered almost hysterical speculation as to the cause."[11]

Investigators found two common environmental factors: garbage and menstruation. Both bears were addicted to garbage; in the vernacular of biologists, they were food-conditioned bears. The bruins had a long history of visiting backcountry camping areas where they obtained food scraps, discarded food containers, and even the remains of fish caught by campers. The second common environmental factor was menstruation. One women was carrying tampons, which led investigators to the conclusion that her period was about to begin. The other woman was actually menstruating.

Although it was well known that garbage attracted grizzlies and often brought them in close proximity with humans, no scientific field research had ever been conducted to determine whether menstrual odors attracted bears or might somehow cause a bear attack. Still, folklore had it that stallions are upset by menstruating women, and menstrual blood had been blamed for triggering shark attacks on women. It wasn't long before the investigators received a number of letters from various people around the country reporting incidents of menstruating women being attacked by a variety of animals.

This reminds me of a 1995 Associated Press news release titled "Smelly Socks Attract Grizzly." After a day of hiking, a hunter in British Columbia took his shoes and socks off to cool his feet. "The bear, he figures, picked up his scent from the smelly socks. 'Within two minutes of me putting my shoes and socks back on and heading back up the trail, the sow came at me full blast from the side,' he said."[12]

This incident doesn't prove smelly socks attract bears any more than a few letters from the public prove animals attack menstruating women. Perhaps the letters sent to Glacier Park provided interesting or amusing reading for biologists and agency officials trying to determine the cause of Glacier's bear attacks; however, they had better evidence to consider:

> On the night of August 13, 1967, two young women [both menstruating], three young men, and one dog were camped together at Trout Lake. The bear approached the camp several times, first at 8:00 P.M. as it was getting dark and after the campers had cooked hot dogs and fish. The bear frightened the campers so they abandoned their campsite and moved their sleeping bags down to the lake. The bear seemed most interested in their food, as had been the case with previous visitors to Trout Lake.
>
> On the bear's final visit, when all the campers were asleep in their sleeping bags, it approached and examined each in turn. Michele Koons was the last person the bear approached. The other four got out of their bags and were jumping and shouting, causing confusion and excitement as they rushed to climb trees. In this atmosphere of noise and excitement, the bear went directly to the one remaining person and almost immediately began tearing into her sleeping bag. . . . Michele couldn't get her zipper undone and could not get out of her bag (USDI 1967). [13]

What initially attracted the bear to the camping area? I'd say it was the bear's previous experience with food and garbage—not menstrual odors. Having the bear so close to the campers set the stage for disaster, but what attracted the bear to Michele Koons? If menstrual odors attract bears, why was the victim the last person the bear visited? Why didn't the bear just ignore the men and go directly for the menstruating women? Why did the bear ignore menstruating woman No. 1 and single out Michele Koons?

Just for the sake of argument, let's say the bear's previous success at obtaining food from hikers at Trout Lake is what initially brought it into the campsite, and the odor of menstruation is the factor that ultimately attracted the bear to Michele Koons. Our next question, then, is, What enticed the bear to attack? Was it menstrual odors? Food odors that saturated her clothes while cooking hot dogs and fish? Michele Koons was also a heavy user of cosmetics. Did the odor of cosmetics cause the attack? What about the shouting and confusion? Did Michele Koons make a sudden movement or a loud noise that caught the bear's attention? How can you pick one factor, isolate it from all other factors, and say, "This is what triggered the attack"?

You can't. Yet the final report on Michele Koon's death mentioned that "[a] number of letters have been received at the Park reporting incidents of women in their monthly period being attacked by various wild animals. It would seem a plausible reason for the attack."[14]

THE AGENCIES REACT

It must have seemed very plausible indeed, because the Park Service and other agencies began to include menstrual warnings in bear brochures and pamphlets distributed to the public. Several Canadian parks also began publishing menstrual warnings.

I'm sure the Park Service and other agencies were genuinely concerned that menstruating women might be at greater risk than other people in bear country. Still, given the complete absence of scientific research on menstrual odors and bears at the time, it seems difficult to justify a decision to publish written menstrual warnings. I'm convinced the primary reason menstrual warnings found their way into print is that government agencies were concerned about protecting themselves from liability for bear attacks. There have been at least seven attempts to sue the U.S. government for negligence in incidents involving bear attacks. In my opinion, the intent of the menstrual warnings was to foil potential lawsuits. In the rare event that a bear attacked a menstruating woman, government lawyers could always tell a judge, "We warned her."

Biologists eventually convinced agencies to remove menstrual warnings from brochures, but then a 1980 study on polar bears by University of Montana graduate student Bruce Cushing brought the issue to the forefront again. I'm going to discuss the study in detail because it provides the only scientific evidence we have that menstrual odors attract bears.[15]

One part of the study tested the responses of polar bears to both menstruating and nonmenstruating women. The bears were kept at a laboratory in Churchill, Manitoba. One at a time, the polar bears were put in a 20-by-20-foot cage in a room equipped with an observation booth. Just outside the bars of the cage, food and odorous items were randomly placed in one of two "fan boxes." Seal oil, human blood, chicken, used tampons, seafood, and other items were placed in the boxes and the fans were run for 20 minutes. Although bears could scent the food, they couldn't reach it. During a 20-minute test period, each bear's behavior was recorded for 10 seconds at the start of every minute.

A "maximum response" was defined as "sniff for most of the test, tracks scent to source, and shows from 5 to 10 minutes of increased activity" such as pacing the cage, pawing, chewing on the bars, chuffing, and sniffing. When a bear sniffed several times and showed increased activity for 2 minutes or less, this was considered a "moderate response." A "minimum response" occurred if the bear sniffed the air three to seven times but didn't move. If there was no movement but the bear sniffed the air ten to twenty times, its response was listed as "minimum-plus."

In tests with women instead of food, the women sat passively by the fan boxes for 20 minutes. The bear in the cage could see the women. With nonmenstruating women, there was one moderate, one minimum-plus, and three minimum responses. With menstruating women, there were six moderate and one minimum response.

Bears did not respond to human blood or unused tampons. Bears did respond to used tampons. There were four maximum responses and one minimum-plus response. One bear slept through the test.

Cushing also observed the reaction of wild bears in an outdoor setting to various food and scents. Plain paper toweling was used to hold 5 milliliters or less of seafood, chicken, blood, and other attractants fixed to forty-two stakes that were widely dispersed in the vicinity of an observation tower. In addition, both used and unused tampons were attached to some of these stakes. The amount of menstrual blood was not measured or controlled. Observers watched forty-five bears approach the stakes 150 times.

When bears approached within 30 yards of the stakes from a down-wind direction, they scented seafood 100 percent of the time, chicken 80 percent, seal oil 73 percent, used tampons 65 percent, and human blood 17 percent. After scenting the attractants, the bears usually investigated the bait stations. The consumption rate was 100 percent for chicken, 92 percent for seal oil, 66 percent for beer, 62 percent for seafood, 54 percent for used tampons, and 13 percent for unused tampons.

Based on the results of these tests, Cushing reached the following conclusions:

> [M]enstrual odors attract bears. . . . [I]t is some aspect peculiar to menstrual blood which elicits this attraction.
>
> Although menstrual odors attract polar bears, we must avoid drawing the simple conclusion that attacks upon menstruating women will occur. The odor test did not take into account the physical presence of human beings [and] the bears, in general, appeared to attempt to avoid or escape the women. This was true in 11 of 12 trials.
>
> Polar bears in the wild would be attracted by menstrual odors, but it is impossible to predict their further actions. Because of other behavioral traits, they may retreat upon discovering the individual, as the test animals in the laboratory usually did. I recommend the following:
>
> - For the present, assume that *all* bears are attracted to menstrual odors, but plan now for investigating this relationship with regard to the other species of bears as soon as possible.
> - Agencies and companies should issue firm warnings and take positive steps to protect human females required to work in bear habitat or who utilize bear habitat for other reasons.

Shortly after the results of Cushing's research were made public, a headline in the October 26, 1980, *Great Falls Tribune* read "Bear Attacks, Menstruation Link Proven."

Copies of the study were distributed for review with Glacier National Park employees. A November 13, 1980, memo from the park's wilderness specialist to the administrative officer said that "it seems timely that we address some potential problems we may now foresee in assigning women employees to backcountry locations."[16]

As you can probably predict, this memo prompted quite a few other memos, and meetings, and high anxiety at high levels of the NPS bureaucracy. There were Equal Employment Opportunity committee meetings and personnel meetings. Lawyers reviewed the facts. Even the director of the NPS wrote memos about women, menstruation, and bears.

Cushing's research was carefully scrutinized. Most people saw one problem right away: Polar bears are 99 percent carnivorous, whereas black and grizzly bears are omnivorous; they consume far more than do polar bears. Another issue was that Cushing's results were based, in part, on how four different polar bears responded to a total of twelve encounters with menstruating and nonmenstruating women—that's a tiny sample size. A group of nine women who worked in Glacier Park pointed out a few other problems:[17]

1. In lab tests, the form of the women was visible to the bear. It's not clear whether the bear was responding to the form of a human or an odor.

2. Cushing suggested that one possible explanation for the bears' interest in used tampons and menstrual odors might be that bears recognize and investigate sexual odors. He emphasized that research would be needed to verify this hypothesis. It can't be assumed that only women have hormonal cycles. Evidence indicates that men have hormonal cycles, too, and any research would need to explore both possibilities.

3. "The methodology employed by Cushing . . . was not scientifically sound." Cushing observed the responses of bears to used tampons. The fluid held within a tampon has a strong odor when it makes contact with bacteria in the air and starts to decompose. Only menstrual blood was tested in the tampons. The results might have been the same with any type of human blood placed in tampons, or human blood in oysters for that matter.

The NPS had doubts about the validity of Cushing's research and apprehension about the legal ramifications of his recommendations. A November 17, 1980, memo from the acting superintendent of Glacier Park to the NPS associate regional director concerning *Backcountry Assignments for Female*

Employees said, "We are hesitant to develop any policy statements on our own. . . . [I]t may be best addressed at least Regionally and possibly at the Washington level. It may also warrant a Solicitor's opinion. Our reaction is that the bear informational handout material should be revised [to] include these findings and be included in all seasonal employee packets. This may serve to ease the liability implications. However, due to EEO and Privacy Act implications, the determination of whether to bring up the subject or not with a supervisor should be left up to the female employee."

The NPS was in a quandary. Because of "liability implications," NPS officials felt they had to warn park visitors that it might be dangerous for menstruating women to travel in bear country. At the same time, the NPS had to tell employees that it was safe for menstruating women to work in bear country. It was clear there would be lawsuits for sexual discrimination if the NPS refused to hire women for jobs in bear country.

A 1981 memo from the director of the NPS to the Rocky Mountain Regional Director said that "based upon . . . the fact that research has not clearly demonstrated that there is a correlation between menstrual odor and bear attraction, we do not believe policy should be established to control assignment of female employees to backcountry areas. In view of the lack of conclusive research, . . . we would be subject of complaints of differential treatment."[18]

In a management directive concerning women in the backcountry, the superintendent of Glacier National Park wrote that the results of Bruce Cushing's polar bear studies "were inconclusive and the applicability of the thesis to Glacier's grizzly and black bears is questionable, and will remain so until further research is conducted."[19]

Although Glacier Park officials told employees that the results of Cushing's research were "inconclusive," their bear literature told the public "odors attract bears . . . menstruating women may choose to stay out of bear country." This leads most people to the conclusion that menstrual odors attract bears. If menstrual odors attract bears, then what choice did women have but to stay out of bear country during their period? As a matter of practical policy, Glacier Park officials were warning you to stay out of bear country during your menstrual period, yet hiring women to work as backcountry rangers. The Flathead National Forest wanted you to stay out of bear country during your menstrual period, yet hired women to work on trail crews in bear country. There were black bears and menstruating women in national forests all over the country, yet only a handful of forests in Montana distributed written menstrual warnings. Women in Yellowstone Park received menstrual warnings; women in Yosemite did not. Glacier, yes. Great Smoky Mountains, no.

Double standards, hypocrisy, and inconsistent policies fostered skepticism about menstrual warnings. As the years went by, a variety of research was done to investigate the theory that menstrual odors attract bears. In *Bear Attacks: Their Cause and Avoidance,* Dr. Stephen Herrero said, "[I]n my analysis of grizzly bear-inflicted injury, I did not find a correlation between attacks on women and any particular stage of their menstrual cycles."[20]

In 1991, longtime black bear biologist Dr. Lynn L. Rogers published a research paper titled "Reactions of Black Bears to Human Menstrual Odors." He did fieldwork, asked the question of hundreds of fellow biologists gathered for a bear conference, and reviewed existing bear literature. His conclusions: "Menstrual odors were essentially ignored by black bears. . . . In an extensive review of black bear attacks across North America, we found no instance of black bears attacking or being attracted to menstruating women."[21]

In 1994, Yellowstone Park's bear management office released an information paper that looked at the statistics on bear-related injuries from 1980 to 1994. Of more than 600,000 visitor-use nights in the backcountry, "Twenty one people were injured by bears within the park. . . . [O]f these 21 injuries, 15 (71%) were men, and 6 (29%) were women. Most (86%) of these injuries involved sudden, close encounters between bear and hiker and were therefore probably unrelated to menstruation. Of the three (14%) incidents where people were injured while camping, two of the injured people were male and one was female. The woman was not menstruating at the time of the attack. There was no evidence linking menstruation to any of these 21 bear attacks."[22]

A COMMONSENSE APPROACH

With all the research that's been done, I believe Caroline Byrd's 1988 master's thesis gives us by far the most thorough analysis of Cushing's research and the whole topic of menstrual odors attracting bears. She warns us that "making the jump from menstruation attracting bears to menstruation causing bear attacks is inappropriate" because so many factors influence the outcome of any encounter between bears and humans.[23]

After reviewing Cushing's field tests with used tampons, seal oil, and other attractants, Byrd says "this still does not answer the question of whether or not bears are attracted to menstruating women. A menstruating woman does not smell like a used tampon. Menstrual flow has an odor only if it has been exposed to the air for some time. Cushing's results suggest [the] need for proper care and disposal of used tampons when in bear country, but they do not clearly indicate that polar bears are attracted to menstruating women."

Byrd also presents a powerful and thoughtful argument that our cultural attitudes toward menstruation predispose people to accept the premise that menstrual odors attract bears. Finally, Byrd did a statistical analysis of hundreds of documented bear encounters and the handful of fatal attacks that have occurred to determine whether bears behaved differently around women and men. Her conclusion? "The question of whether menstruating women attract bears has not been answered. . . . Statistical analyses of bear/human encounters seem to indicate that bears do not respond significantly differently to men or women. Case by case analyses do not reveal menstruation playing a role in human female's encounters with bears, but there is much missing and unknowable information. Given the nature of the question, it cannot be said with confidence that bears are, or are not attracted to menstrual odors."

In other words, statistics tell us that menstrual odors don't attract bears, or that the attractiveness of menstrual (and other) odors is usually offset by a bear's reluctance to get too close to people. Furthermore, given the nature of grizzly bears, it's extremely difficult to do field tests that prove menstrual odors don't attract grizzlies. We'll never be 100 percent sure about these things. Based on all the evidence we have about menstruation and bears, I offer the following thoughts and advice:

1. Use unscented or lightly scented tampons or pads rather than the heavily scented type.
2. Use OB or similar tampons for less odorous byproducts from plastic and cardboard applicators.
3. Wash your hands after changing and handling tampons or pads.
4. Store used tampons or pads as carefully as you store food, garbage, and other odorous items. Use bear cans or hang them with your garbage at least 4 feet from a tree trunk and 10 feet off the ground. As an extra precaution, keep used tampons or pads in air-tight resealable plastic bags.
5. Treat soiled garments (underwear, etc.) as you would food and garbage.
6. Do not bury pads or tampons in the backcountry. Bears have

keen noses. They might smell buried pads or tampons as they would garbage and dig them up.

7. If you decide to burn used tampons to *reduce* (not eliminate) odors, remove charred remains of them from the fire pit and store them with other garbage. Bear literature often says you can burn used tampons in a hot fire, but a biologist with the Alaska Department of Fish and Game tried that and found "it's impossible." There's no way you can completely burn a used tampon.

8. Use internal tampons rather than external pads. If this is a health concern and you decide to use external pads, be aware that this will cause one additional odor a bear might notice. Every odor counts in bear country. It doesn't matter whether you put on strawberry-scented lip balm before you go to bed at night or you unknowingly spill fruit juice on the sleeve of the shirt you're sleeping in. Every odor counts. To me, this just emphasizes the need to keep a clean camp and do everything right in bear country.

Once Cushing's polar bear research was released, it's easy to understand why the agencies felt compelled to put some sort of menstrual information in bear brochures; they just did a lousy job of it. They overreacted. The IGBC's *Women in Bear Country* states that "bears can sense fear." For almost thirty years, millions of visitors to national parks and forests have been handed brochures and pamphlets with threatening menstrual warnings that cause women to fear bears. Fortunately, that situation is changing. IGBC headquarters is trying to persuade all IGBC members to update their bear brochures. Yellowstone already has its excellent information paper titled *Bears and Menstruating Women*. Women who might have been put off by scary menstrual warnings in the past can now get accurate facts and enjoy bear country.

SEX IN THE WILD

Any sexual odor may attract or at least interest a bear.
—*Paul Schullery,* The Bears of Yellowstone, *1986*

When I was at the McNeil River State Game Sanctuary watching bears with a small group of people led by Alaska Department of Fish and Game biologist Derek Stonorov, I mentioned that some bear brochures claim that human sexual behavior may attract bears.

Derek lives in Homer, Alaska, a small town featured in Tom Bodett's *The End of the Road*. It's an hour's flight from the end of the road to McNeil, where Derek escorts ten people a day to McNeil River Falls, home of the greatest concentration of brown bears on earth. As many as sixty-eight bears at a time have been seen feeding on chum salmon at the falls. Derek has been at McNeil on and off since the early 1970s, when he wrote his master's thesis on bear behavior. Derek knows bears. He keeps up on scientific bear literature. But because Derek lives at the end of the road, I wasn't surprised he hadn't heard about sex warnings in the Lower 48 states. When I mentioned the sex warnings, Derek gave me a quizzical look and asked, "Are you serious?"

"Yep," I said, "but I've never found any studies on the topic. I've asked the agencies that give sex warnings for references. I've asked more than once. No response. What a great research project for an intrepid grad student."

To the amusement of our entire group, Derek began thinking out loud.

"Can you imagine the exit survey for backpackers leaving bear country. Excuse me, did you engage in sex? Are either of you especially vocal? Do you tend to, ah, thrash around quite a bit? Did you use condoms?"

If you think about it, we're often told to make noise to avoid surprising bears; during sex, people make all kinds of noise. You're supposed to shout at a black bear entering your camp; during sex, some people shout and yell. If you're in a close-up encounter with a grizzly, you should talk quietly to the bear; after sex, people often talk quietly with each other. Maybe human sexual activity deters bears. Maybe it attracts them. Maybe smelly socks attract bears. Nobody knows. And because nobody knows, agencies have no justification for publishing written warnings that say "human sexual practices may attract bears."

I can't help wondering if "just say no" to sex in the wild is another way of saying you don't want your tent to smell like Cupid's gym. Now that's a legitimate concern. Fluids are also a legitimate concern. If you're so unimaginative or inexperienced you can't think of any human sexual practices that will keep odors to a minimum and eliminate liquids, don't have sex in bear country until you call Dr. Ruth.

Cooking and Food Storage

To him almost everything is food except granite.

—*John Muir, "Bears," 1901*

John Muir was wrong. When it comes to natural foods, bears are rather finicky. Out of 1,000 types of plants in a given area, they might only consume 100 to 250, and each of those will be eaten during a particular season. Yet as my friend Mark Jefferson discovered on a recent kayaking trip in Southeast Alaska, bears will try to taste almost anything once.

Jefferson is a lunatic of sorts, a beady-eyed accountant–turned–computer programmer who's fond of slightly crazed outdoor adventures. During a recent Alaskan kayak trip, Jefferson left his campsite for "a minute" and, when he returned a half-hour later, the black bear that had destroyed his tent was now casually picking through the debris. Jefferson chased the bear off and surveyed the damage. There were gaping holes in his tent, insulation from his sleeping bag adorned the beach grass and nearby alders, and all of his food had been eaten, but what really annoyed Jefferson is that the bear had bitten his portable Macintosh computer. "I could see indents and scratches from his teeth," Mark told me.

I didn't ask Mark why he took a computer with him on a kayaking trip in Alaska—as I mentioned earlier, he's a lunatic—but this "modern-day Mac attack" illustrates that bears will taste-test almost anything.

HOW BEARS BECOME FOOD-CONDITIONED

Because bears are curious, intelligent, powerful, and endlessly searching for food, improper food storage is the root cause of many conflicts and confrontations between bears and humans. State and federal land agencies publish brochures that include slogans like "a fed bear is a dead bear" or "garbage kills bears," and these slogans often prove true. Hikers and active outdoors people often think it's other people—the suburban family "camping" in a 38-foot-long air-conditioned RV—who corrupt bears with hot dogs and chips, but a 1980 study in Yosemite National Park found that while

92 percent of all backpackers said they stored their food correctly only 3 percent actually did.[24]

The chain of events that turns fed bears into dead bears is depressingly familiar to bear aficionados. A family from Anywhere USA rents an RV and drives to Banff National Park in Alberta, Canada. They leave a bag of groceries on the picnic table when they go to an evening ranger talk. When they return, scraps of paper and plastic are strewn everywhere, but all the fixings for turkey sandwiches are gone, eaten, consumed by a black bear that now associates this campground area with food. A day later, the bear returns, only this time there are people watching. The bear is nervous. It would probably run if someone shouted or took a quick step toward it. Instead, someone tosses the bear a bag of potato chips. Now the bear associates both the campground and people with food. The next time it returns, banging together pots and pans probably won't deter the bear. Even if you blew off firecrackers, the bear might not leave, at least not for long. It's been rewarded with food and it's coming back for more. At this particular campground, a certain tolerance for humans replaces the bear's initial caution around people. It could be more likely to risk getting close to people at other locations, too.

This bear doesn't have long to live. Maybe it will wander into a hunter's camp outside the park and get shot. It might start approaching backpackers and be "removed from the population" by a land management agency. Someone at the campground might try to grab food back from the bear and get cuffed in retaliation. If a person is seriously injured, or sometimes just scared, we retaliate by killing the bear. Fed bears are often dead bears.

The big picture here is that bears weigh positive gains (food) versus the risk of injury, hassles with people, and other negative factors. When the positive outweighs the negative, the bear will seek food. When the negative outweighs the positive, the bear will move on. Storing food properly is the single most important thing you can do to prevent conflicts between bears and humans.

I've heard people whine about how much trouble it is to store food in bear country, but if you don't use the same basic techniques when camping on the Havasupai Reservation in the Grand Canyon, ringtails will get your food. Raccoons and skunks will raid your food cache in places like Kentucky and Tennessee. Regardless of where you camp, some precautions will probably be necessary to protect your food from hungry critters.

Stern warnings about bears, food, and garbage have given many people the impression that all bears wander around the woods dreaming of noodle soup and chocolate bars. They don't. Still, any new or interesting odor can attract a naturally curious bear, and the big problem is that while there may be a few places in Alaska and Canada where bears have never tasted human food, you have to assume the worst. You have to operate on the principle that most bears in North America associate humans with food. You can't lose with this approach. If you're visiting a place where bears are food-conditioned, proper food storage techniques will protect your precious food cache from hungry, inquisitive bears. If the bears in your area have never sampled human food, yours won't be the first, and you won't be responsible for the death of a bear or a human injury. Remember: Once bears get food from humans, they're addicts, and most addicts die young.

COOKING

DONT COOK—EAT COLD FOOD

If a bubbling pot of Coq au Vin smells good to you, imagine how interesting it smells to every bear near your camp. There's an easy way to eliminate cooking odors, greatly reduce food storage problems, and just make life afield simpler: *Eat cold food.* Most of us are lucky to get away for weekend or overnight hikes, and a day or two of dried fruit and hippie granola won't compromise an enjoyable getaway. In *Wilderness Camping,* Denton W. Crocker tells of eating a steady diet of cold food for almost two weeks.[25] He didn't get ridiculously tired of his cold food diet, and he found the freedom from pots and pans and cooking and cleaning to be quite liberating. He watched sunsets rather than washing dishes. Eating cold food is the easiest, most effective, and most commonly overlooked method of reducing food odors. It's not for everyone, though—hot chocolate and hot soup are far more satisfying on a cold, wet day than dehydrated prunes—but it really does help minimize the potential for food-related problems in bear country.

IF YOU DO COOK . . .

Although many people think the main reason behind proper food storage is that you don't want a bear sniffing around your food cache at night, in Denali National Park's backcountry the element of surprise has been the leading factor in how bears have received food rewards during the past decade. Backcountry campers are advised to cook in the open where visibility is good. This gives you time to react if you see a bear approaching. Before you start cooking, take a look around and ask yourself, What's the plan if a bear comes into camp? If you keep a large resealable plastic bag near your cooksite, it's handy for storing bits of food and trash that might otherwise hit the ground, and you could dump a hot, half-cooked meal into it if necessary. Zip. Put it in your bear can or take it with you rather than allowing a bear to dine on it.

Before you start cooking, though, you need to consider other things before you even set out on a trip. If you do a lot of winter camping, you'll have to cook in your tent and it will be permeated with food odors. A thorough washing before the summer season will remove some odors, but it's better to have a different tent that you have never cooked in for summer camping in bear country. You should also carefully plan food quantities before you leave home, so you don't have to store leftovers while in bear country.

Once you arrive at your campsite, you need to set it up properly. Your cooking area should be a minimum of 100 yards downwind from your sleeping area, but check local requirements for the proper distance. You'll also need to check locally for the correct arrangement for your food storage area–cooking area–sleeping area. Some parks require a triangular arrangement with your sleeping area on the point and your food storage and cooking areas at the base. Other parks tell people to keep their sleeping area 100 yards or more from a combination cooking area–food storage area. Remember that cool air tends to flow downslope at night, so store your food downwind and downslope. Sea kayakers in coastal waters should cook below the high tide line, and wash their pots, dishes, and utensils by the shore in saltwater.

Once you do begin your meal, the following pointers should be kept in mind:

- Whether you're cooking along the coast of the ocean or a high mountain meadow, keep an open resealable plastic bag near your stove. This will help you resist the temptation of flicking small bits of food on the ground.
- Try to cook your evening meal in one location a few hours before dark and then move on to the place where you plan to sleep.
- Cooking can be a chaotic affair, with spices here, soy sauce there, your main dish on the stove, and other food scattered everywhere. Once you're ready to start cooking, get all your food together in one place so you can grab it quickly if a bear ambles into the kitchen. Only take out the food that's needed. Don't eat picnic-style.
- Avoid bacon, sausage, fish, and other smelly food. In addition

to giving off strong odors while cooking, the smell permeates your clothing.

- Never, never, never leave cooking food unattended.
- At home, we're all well-mannered people so we don't wipe our hands on our pants while we're cooking and eating. That's what washclothes and napkins are for, right? When we're camping, our Emily Post etiquette sometimes lapses. It's not a good idea to wipe your hands or—gasp—kitchen utensils on your clothes when you're camping in bear country. Keep a handkerchief handy for wiping your hands.

After you're done cooking, wash dishes immediately after each use. If there are a lot of food particles in the dishwater, dispose of it properly at least 100 yards from camp. Wash your hands and face thoroughly after meals and before going to sleep. Don't wash yourself or your dishes in freshwater lakes or streams.

Don't sleep in the same clothes you wore while cooking. Hang your cooking clothes in plastic bags. Food odors tend to permeate clothes, so you might want to smoke them over a fistful of sage, pine, or some other aromatic plant. Rinse out your handkerchief or dish rag and store it with your food and garbage.

FOOD STORAGE

When you store food, it might pay to make a game of it and pretend you're playing keep-away from Yosemite's intelligent and well-educated black bears. In Yosemite, some people use the counterbalance method of hanging food way out on a skinny tree limb that won't support the weight of an adult bear. It doesn't always work. People have witnessed bears get as close as they can and then make a flying leap at their food sack. In other cases, people have parked their classic Volkswagen bug at a trailhead, rolled the windows up tight, and locked it before going for a day hike. While they were hiking, a bear climbed up on the Volkswagen's roof and hopped up and down a few times until air pressure popped open the doors. If you can prevent a Yosemite bear from getting your food, you can probably foil any bear.

First, study the land and pick a food storage site that's not attractive to bears. Don't store food right beside trails, on the edge of a meadow, or near berry patches or other obvious sources of food. Try to pick a place that's in the open so you can examine it from a safe distance. I like to be able to see my food cache from my tent.

Once you've selected a good site, don't make the same mistake that has resulted in many dead bears and injured hunters; they kill an elk late in the evening, but, with darkness approaching, there's no time to quarter it and pack it back to camp. They just gut it and hang the whole carcass from a tree. When they return to collect "their" trophy the next morning, they casually walk into a grizzly bear that fed on the gut pile at night. Charge. Bang. Injured hunter, dead bear.

Don't be a yahoo. Before you begin walking toward your food cache in the morning, use binoculars to examine it. Study the surrounding area for bears. Take a few minutes. Look for ravens and other scavengers that might suggest your food has been strewn around. Don't make your approach until you're certain there are no bears around, and make a bit of noise just to be sure.

Here are a few examples of food, garbage, and odorous items used for preparing and/or eating food that must be properly stored whenever they're not in use.

- **All human food**
- **Fresh fish**
- **Wine, beer, soda: any full or empty beverage can**
- **Water bottles that contained drink mixes and all plastic bottles**
- **Stoves and fuel**
- **Ice chests, silverware, cooking utensils**
- **Cooking clothes**
- **Lotions, ointments, sunscreens, and all other toiletries**
- **Soap, shampoo, medications**
- **Horse and dog feed**
- **Trash and garbage**

And what about your pack? Whenever possible, I try to hang my pack. I'm always concerned that carrying food in the pack somehow left food odors in it. I once had ground squirrels in Glacier Park chew apart my salty, sweat-soaked shoulder straps. If you can't hang your pack, don't bring it in your tent at night. Unzip all the pockets, empty them, leave them open, and leave your pack outside the tent.

FOOD STORAGE EQUIPMENT
Whoever invented resealable plastic bags did the backpacking community a big favor, and I couldn't survive in the backcountry without garbage bags.

The dry bags used by kayakers and canoeists are much sturdier than garbage bags, and bear-resistant food containers are the ultimate food storage device. You'll need light rope or parachute cord for hanging your food from trees. When people think about food storage, they're usually wondering how they can keep their food safe at night. Remember that you need to keep food and food odors away from your clothing, tent, and pack, too. That's why resealable plastic bags and garbage bags are so handy.

Bear-resistant food containers are heavy-duty ABS plastic cylinders about the size and shape of a summer sleeping bag in a stuff sack. People who use them regularly just call them bear cans. The one company that manufactures bear cans for hikers makes a Base Camp model, which is 18 inches long by 8 inches in diameter, and a Backpacker, which is 12 inches long by 8 inches in diameter. Bears can't get their jaws around them or undo the lids, which are secured with two flat-head screws that fit flush with the surface of the container. You can tighten the screws with a coin, a knife, or whatever's handy. Bear cans are sleek, smooth, and damn near indestructible. The manufacturer can't say they're bear-proof—that's an invitation for a lawsuit—but until bears learn how to use Swiss army knives, a properly secured bear can will prevent grizzlies or black bears from getting at the food inside. They make good camp stools, too. That's the good news.

The bad news is that bear cans are heavy, clumsy, clunky things with a relatively small storage capacity. Rectangular blocks of cheese or even those square little vegetable bullion cubes just weren't designed to fit into a perfectly round cylinder. You have to mash food into bear cans. Even then, you always waste a bit of space. The Backpacker model has a volume of 560 cubic inches and carries about 5 to 6 days worth of freeze-dried or dehydrated food for one person. It weighs 2.9 pounds empty. An empty Base Camp model weighs 5 pounds.

Because bear cans are big and heavy, they don't ride well when strapped to the outside of a pack. Try to put them inside your pack, and strap lightweight, bulky items on the outside. It's usually easy to get a bear can into the hatch of a sea kayak, but sometimes you have to leave a bit of space inside the hold, maneuver the bear can in, and then pack around it. Bear cans don't float, and they're not watertight, so store them upside down so rain doesn't leak in. Don't use them as a stand for your stove, because they'll melt. Bears can't break them but you can—the tabs are the weak spot. It's easy to break the tabs off the lid. The manufacturer does make a nylon carrying case with an assortment of buckles and D rings that allow you to strap the containers on the outside of your pack or vessel. The carrying case also gives you a means of hanging the container from trees, a requirement in some parks, forests, and recreation areas.

Bear cans are not only heavy and ungainly, they're expensive. Prices begin at $78, and carrying cases are an additional $16–18. Despite the cost, size, and weight of bear cans, they have one redeeming quality—they work. They really work. After the National Park Service began requiring backpackers to use bear cans in Denali in 1984, there was a 95 percent reduction in bears obtaining food from backpackers and an 88 percent decrease in property damage in the backcountry. As of 1995, not a single bear had broken into the "new" model bear cans made by Garcia Machine (14097 Avenue 272, Visalia, CA 93292; (209) 732-3785).

If you want to reduce food odors that might attract bears, prevent bears from getting into your food, and reduce the odds that you'll have a bear in camp at night, use a bear can.

HANGING FOOD, GARBAGE, AND ODOROUS ITEMS
As a general rule, your food should be hung at least 10 feet off the ground and 4 feet away from the tree trunk, but check local requirements. In some parks and forests, hanging your food out of reach of bears is easy: use the cables, crossbars, or food poles generously provided by agencies such as the Park Service and Forest Service. Don't tie off your rope or cord on support poles because bears will sometimes climb those poles, bump the rope, see your food bag move, and make the connection.

If you're on your own, the counterbalance technique is the best method for hanging your food from a tree. It merely forestalls the inevitable in Yosemite, but it will foil bears almost anywhere else. The idea is to hang two food sacks of equal weight way out on a tree branch where bears can't reach them. The main problem with the counterbalance technique is finding the right tree with the right branch. Your first requirement is a "live" branch at least 15 feet above the ground. The branch must be strong enough to support the weight of your food but not sturdy enough for a bear cub to walk on. You're looking for a branch about 4 to 5 inches in diameter at the base and only 1 inch in diameter at the point where you hang your food.

With the counterbalance method, your food must be at least 10 feet above the ground and 10 feet away from the tree trunk. You want your food sacks to hang about 5 feet below the branch.

1. Begin by putting a rock or weight of some sort in a sock, tying a rope to it, and throwing it over the branch. Move the rope as

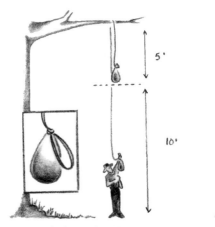

Counterbalance food hanging method

far out toward the end of the branch as possible. Some manufacturers now make "bear bags" with a food sack on one end of the cord, and a smaller sack to hold a weight at the other end. Wearing gloves will prevent rope burns. Thick rope is less likely to tangle.

2. Your food should be in two sacks or containers of equal weight. They shouldn't weigh more than 10 pounds each because an inch-thick branch won't support more than 20 pounds.

3. Tie one end of the rope around the neck of one sack, securing it firmly. Tie a loop in the rope near your sack for retrieving your food later. Hoist the sack all the way up to the branch by pulling on the free end of the rope. Now reach up and tie your second food sack as high up on the rope as you can. Again, tie a secure loop in the rope near the second sack. Put any excess rope into the sack.

4. Toss the sack into position or push it up with a stick so the sacks are balanced over the branch. Don't forget: A 6-foot-tall person will need a 5- to-6-foot-long stick to hook the loop on the food sacks when it's time to retrieve them.

Properly executed, this technique will foil most bears, raccoons, and other late night raiders—but it's not bear-proof in places like Yosemite. It will buy you time, that's all. If you're lucky, you'll hear the bear(s) and have time to get out of your sleeping bag and take action before your food is gone.

You can also suspend a food bag on a rope strung between two trees conveniently located about 23 feet apart. You'll need 100 feet or more of ⅛-inch or larger nylon rope, a weight of some sort for throwing the rope over tree limbs, and a carabiner or short piece of nylon cord for attaching your food sack to the rope.

1. Throw the weighted end of your rope over a limb about 17 feet high. Lower the weight to the ground. Tie off the other end of the line as high up as you can reach on the base of tree No. 1.
2. Now pull all your slack over the limb, run the rope along the ground toward tree No. 2, and set your food sack on the rope a little more than halfway between tree No. 1 and tree No. 2. Then throw the weighted end of the rope over a 17-foot-high limb on tree No. 2.
3. Attach your food bag so it will be in the middle of the line between the trees.
4. Hoist up your food bag and tie off the rope on tree No. 2. The food should be about 12 feet above the ground.

This system is fairly effective with novice bears. Experienced food robbers will wonder why you didn't set up a table with silverware for them.

Years of experience in Denali and other national parks have proven that properly secured bear resistant food containers work. (Richard Garcia)

They'll simply rip off the line from the tree trunk and feast on your food when it falls down.

One last technique is to throw a line over a limb, suspend your food 12 feet above ground and 5 feet below the limb, and then tie the line off as high up on the tree trunk as you can reach. This technique is better than nothing with inexperienced bears, and it helps keep mice, squirrels, and other pests out of your food.

When your food is 12 feet high, wind will disperse the scent more than if it were on the ground. Keep your food in plastic bags to reduce odors.

Hanging food from tree branches can test your patience. It's easy to draw an illustration showing the perfect branch, but finding one in the field is another matter. You settle for a branch that looks all right, but a tangle of other branches is in the way. Your aim is a little off and you're snagged on the wrong branch. You try again and this toss falls short. Then you hit the branch. Curses. When you finally manage to toss your rope over a limb, it's too close to the tree trunk and little nubs on the limb prevent you from moving the rope out where it should be. Reading step-by-step instructions for hanging food is far easier than doing it in the field; however, you need to be as persistent as the bears that might try getting your food.

STORING FOOD ON THE GROUND

If you're camping above timberline or exploring remote, treeless areas of Alaska and Canada where you have no choice but to store your food on the ground, I recommend using bear cans whenever possible. I know, I know— bear cans are too big and bulky and heavy. You can't fit enough food inside for extended trips. Sorry, a generation of hikers in Denali National Park has found ways to fit their food in bear cans and you can, too. Remember— before Denali National Park started requiring the use of bear cans, bears often found food that was cached on the ground in plastic bags.

What if bear cans are wholly impractical? Let's say you're taking a three-week hike in the Arctic National Wildlife Refuge. Bring the least odorous foods practical, double-bag everything, and then stash it at least 100 yards from your tent. You could also put food in dry bags and submerge them by weighting them with a few rocks. Just be sure to look along the shore for bear trails and make sure the water is fairly deep. Every summer hikers in Yellowstone put six-packs of beer and soda in creeks to cool it, and every summer bears find it.[26] Avoid trails and areas where there are bear foods. If there are cliffs or big boulders nearby, it might be possible to hang your food bag out of reach. Bears, however, are much better at scaling cliffs than the average person. You'd have to be a skilled rock climber to reach places a bear can't. Try to put your food in a place that's visible from your tent—if you happen to notice wolves, foxes, or other curious critters investigating your cache, you can frighten them away.

FOOD STORAGE WHILE CAR CAMPING

Sometimes we find ourselves spending the night in a car campground by a trailhead or using a car campground as a base camp for exploring a national forest or park. You have to be extra careful at car campgrounds in bear country. They're often situated in prime bear habitat. As a generalization, car campers tend to have a cavalier attitude about bears. They leave out ice chests filled with food. They spill food on picnic tables and don't clean it up. All too often people have allowed bears to obtain food here in the past, so food-conditioned bears might visit the campground again. If the campground's garbage cans are overflowing, or if the garbage cans aren't bearproof, you should consider camping somewhere else.

Parks such as Yosemite provide bear-proof metal storage boxes/lockers and bear-proof garbage cans. Use them. An alarming number of people don't. If bear-proof metal storage boxes are not available, put all food and related supplies in the trunk of your car. Some bears know that ice chests and tin cans contain food, so don't tempt a bear by leaving them in plain sight on the back seat of your car. If your vehicle doesn't have a trunk, cover all food and food-related items with a blanket or something so bears can't see them. Keep your windows tightly closed. If you crack your window open a quarter of an inch, bears can hook their claws inside and pull out your window. Lock your doors. Bears can easily rip down window frames to get at food they see inside your car. They pry and push and pull to test the strength of any edge or corner they can get a grip on.

When it's practical, seal food in air-tight containers or plastic bags to minimize odors. Never leave your camp unattended if food is not stored safely. Not all bears are nocturnal raiders; some bears make daytime forays into camps. Store your food properly day and night. Put your trash in bearproof dumpsters and garbage cans frequently. Keep a clean camp.

GARBAGE

Pack it in, pack it out. Make it easy on yourself by eliminating useless packaging material when you pack for your trip. Never bury garbage. Bears will smell it and dig it up. If campfires are allowed and you attempt to burn garbage, you'll still have to dig every charred scrap of food and aluminum foil out of the ashes and pack it out. Don't take any chances. You can never be certain that complete combustion has destroyed every trace of food and food odors. The packaging for hot chocolate, instant soup, and freeze-dried food does not burn completely. Some heavily used backcountry areas have pit toilets; don't throw any food or garbage in pit toilets because bears might tip them over to get the food and in your next life you'll be given the duty of cleaning up the mess.

BOATERS

You should always think of a beach as a bear trail and assume that bears will investigate anything you leave on the trail. Here in Alaska, I've watched bears paw and gnaw at outboard engines. They're fond of petroleum products. They love bouncing up and down on inflatable rubber rafts. They bite them too, and that's usually the coup de grace. When marker buoys for crab pots wash ashore, bears chew on them and bat them around. They like things that "give." They also pick up oars and paddles in their mouth and shake them. Tracks on the beach have shown me that bears will make a big detour to check out a kayak dragged ashore above the high tide line. Don't tempt curious bears by leaving food in your kayak or stored beneath your canoe. There's a chance the bear will casually rip apart your kayak to get at a bag of dried fruit you accidentally left behind your seat. They can flip your canoe over like it's a toy. Once you're on shore, keep food away from your canoe or kayak to minimize the risk that a bear will damage it.

BREAKING THE RULES

I've come across two books and one magazine article that advise people to violate food storage rules. Their message is: Don't bother with the whole rigmarole of hanging your food from a tree—just put it in a garbage bag and cache it on the ground a good, safe distance from your campsite.

I object, I object, I object. The rationale for breaking the rules is that in popular places like Minnesota's Boundary Waters Canoe Area bears constantly check out campsites. Many campsites have only one really good tree for hanging food, and the bears know where it is. If you don't hang your food just right, bears will get it. Even if you do hang your food properly, you might find out the hard way that the tree branch you selected was actually less than perfect. To outsmart camp bears, don't put your food where everyone else does. Instead, put odor-free food in plastic bags and stash them on the ground well away from your campsite, game paths, and hiking trails.

After giving you this advice, the authors go on to say that in twenty years of camping they've never had a bear get into their food. And I believe them. But what would happen if the Forest Service told every camper in the Boundary Waters Canoe Area, "Forget about hanging your food from trees. Use Joe Rebel's time-proven food storage techniques."

My guess is that by the end of one season, there would be a well-established path leading from each campsite to the one and only "secret spot" where 90 percent of all campers hid their food. Bears would figure out the system and follow the path to the campers' food. Just because you tell people to store their food a 100 yards or more from camp doesn't mean they're going to do it. (Remember that only 3 percent of Yosemite's backcountry users stored their food properly.) Human nature being what it is, a lot of people camping in the Boundary Waters Canoe Area would throw their food on the ground 50 or 25 yards from camp. Before long, bears would figure out that a methodical search within 50 yards of any campsite would probably lead to a bag of goodies. (When grizzlies hunt elk calves in Yellowstone, cow elk try to lead the bear away while their almost scentless calves lie still on the ground. Some grizzlies ignore the cows and conduct a gridlike search for the calves.)[27]

In the unlikely event that every camping party of the summer did walk off in a different direction to store their food, all the brush, shrubs, and trees around the campsite would be trampled. From the air, every campsite would look like a bomb crater. Joe Rebel's time-proven food storage techniques might work for one person, but as a public policy it would be a disaster.

The agencies are in a tough position. Once the decision is made to allow large numbers of people to camp overnight in bear country, food storage is a critical issue. Joe Rebel's food storage plan won't work, yet it's true that finding the perfect tree to hang food is difficult. Bear cans are one solution to this problem. Denali and other parks now require backcountry users to lug around bear cans. Yellowstone Park has installed bear poles for hanging food at backcountry campsites. They detract from the wilderness. You hike for miles to get away from cars and buildings and human artifacts, and when you arrive at your campsite—yuck—there's this butt-ugly bear pole. Park administrators don't like paying for them and backcountry rangers don't like looking at them any more than you or I, but what are the alternatives? If you've got a better idea for storing food than the current system, land management agencies would love to hear about it.

Always think of the big picture when confronted with burdensome food storage regulations. I believe the situation we now have in places like the Boundary Waters Canoe Area or the Bob Marshall Wilderness Area is analogous to Yellowstone in the 1950s. Back then, beggar bears were a regular feature along the roadside. They also rummaged through the campgrounds. The National Park Service installed bear-proof garbage cans and launched an intensive educational campaign. Bears promptly began looking for food in hotels, campgrounds, and other developed areas. Dozens, some say hundreds, of bears were killed, but eventually people stopped feeding bears. The mama bears that survived were no longer rewarded for visiting campgrounds, and their cubs never picked up this habit. Now bears no longer associate the roads or campgrounds with food. It takes at least a generation or two for efforts like this to succeed. It takes constant vigilance, because in years when natural foods are scarce, even bears that have never tasted human food before are more likely to check out campgrounds and other human settlements for food. In the long run, proper food storage makes the woods a better place for bears and us.

Camping and Travel Tips

CAMPING

Campsite selection is critically important. Some campsites where people have traditionally preferred to pitch their tents—lakeshores, stream bottoms, on the edge of alpine meadows—are places bears prefer, as well. Humans like these campsites because they're on or near trails, and for the convenience of nearby water. Bears like these places because they're on or near trails, and for the convenience of nearby food. If you're in mountainous country, don't camp on saddles or ridges that are gentle enough to serve as natural travel corridors. Where forests and meadows meet, bears tend to stick to the edge of the meadow or travel just inside the cover of the forest. These are bad places to camp. You're better off deep in the forest or way out in the open. Don't pitch your tent where bears feed, rest, or travel regularly.

In some parks you don't get to choose your campsite—backcountry users in Yellowstone and some other parks are required to stay in designated sites. Beware. These sites were not selected with bears in mind. The National Park Service simply made traditional campsites (some dating from the 1870s) into designated sites. Traditionally, people have camped in all the wrong places. If you're not familiar with the country where you'll be camping, take a good look at a topo map and ask questions. How far back is my campsite from the lakeshore? How close am I to that stream? Are there any spawning fish in the stream? After studying a topo map and asking a few pointed questions, you might decide to select a different campsite.

When you camp in a designated site, you risk paying for the sins of others who camped there before you. Did they spill food when they were cooking fish over an open fire? Did they lose a tube of toothpaste that was later discovered by a bear who now pays regular visits to your designated site? You might see digging or other evidence that a bear has visited this camp. You might not. Usually, there's no way of knowing.

The good news about designated sites is that some are equipped with bear poles, food storage lockers, or cables for hanging your food safely from a tree. This reduces the risk that a bear visited your site and was rewarded with food.

Set up camp well before dark so you're not forced to pitch your tent in a bad location just because you ran out of daylight. Bears use hiking trails at night, so don't set up camp right next to a main thoroughfare.

Coastal kayakers should avoid a narrow beach backed by cliffs or a high, steep slope. A bear walking along the shore would be funneled right through your camp. Stay a couple hundred feet away from streams as well as from the meadows and beach flats near freshwater streams. Spawning fish may attract bears to these areas, and the gurgling water makes it difficult to hear. You can often see bad campsites from the water.

For a good campsite, look for a wide beach. The forest behind it should be flat or have a gentle uphill slope. Scout the area before setting up camp. Sometimes there are game trails just inside the forest. Bear trails are much wider than deer trails. If you pitch your tent in an open area that's either in or adjacent to the beach zone, you'll have good visibility, and bears walking along the shore or just inside the forest won't walk right into your camp. If you decide to camp in the forest, go well back into the trees—100 yards or more. Don't camp right where the beach meets the shore because bears tend to walk in this transition zone.

Sleeping under the stars is not a good idea in grizzly country. While there have been a few cases where bears pulled sleeping people from tents, there are more cases where bears nailed people sleeping under the stars. The flimsy nylon walls of a tent aren't a physical barrier to bears; however, bears tend to approach strange new objects cautiously. There's a chance you could wake up at night and hear a bear outside your tent. Predatory attacks by grizzlies occur most often at night; if this should happen, take action:

1. Fight the urge to quietly shrink down into your sleeping bag.
2. Talk softly to the bear so it can identify you as a human being.
3. If you have pepper spray, get it ready (see the chapter "Guns and Pepper Spray").
4. Pick up your flashlight, quickly unzip your tent door, turn on your flashlight, and shine it at the bear to momentarily blind it.
5. If the bear does not take off, whoop, holler, and make noise, or spray it with pepper spray if you have it.

Whether the bear is after you or your food, you want to get it out of there.

> Unlike grizzly bear mothers, black bear mothers seldom attack
> people in defense of cubs. . . . [R]esearchers who routinely capture
> cubs by chasing them up trees have not been attacked even when
> they have held screaming cubs. The ferocity of mother black bears is
> one of the biggest misconceptions about this species.
> —*Lynn L. Rogers,* Watchable Wildlife: The Black Bear, *1992*

The chances of being charged by a black bear are zilch unless you're a biologist working closely with bears or a ninny feeding roadside bears in a national park. On the other hand, most skirmishes with grizzly bears occur when people inadvertently startle a grizzly at close range. It's often noted that, statistically, the odds of being killed while driving in a place like Yellowstone or Banff are far greater than the odds of being killed by a bear while hiking in the backcountry. This just proves the adage that statistics are meaningless. Few people lose any sleep over the thought of dying in a car wreck—we didn't evolve to fear this type of danger—but the idea of being attacked by a bear triggers an ancient and visceral fear in all of us.

A great deal of the advice that follows is intended specifically for people traveling in grizzly country, but some topics (like taking dogs afield) apply to both black and grizzly bears. However, even if you're never going to travel in grizzly country, you might want to take a look at both of the following sections.

GENERAL PRECAUTIONS

Dogs: Most bear literature tells you to leave your dog at home or keep it on a leash. The concern is that your dog will encounter a bear, get it all riled up, and then come running back to you with the bear in pursuit. The assumption is that you have an untrained, ill-mannered mutt. All too often that's an accurate assumption; however, some people have well-trained dogs that are an asset in bear country. These dogs can detect bears and warn you of their presence long before you'd know there was a bear about, especially at night.

Before you enter bear country with your dog, first check on local regulations. In many national parks, dogs are prohibited on trails and in the backcountry. Other places have leash laws. All land management agencies have different rules and regulations for different areas; be familiar with local requirements. Try to be realistic about your dog's training and behavior. There have been only a handful of incidents when a dog led an angry bear back to its owner, so the purpose of leash laws really isn't to protect you and your dog from bears. Instead, leash laws are meant to protect wildlife and other people from your dog. If you allow your untrained dog to run loose in the backcountry—especially backcountry areas with leash laws—expect confrontations with people who will be tempted to kick your dog and test-fire their pepper spray at its rude and inconsiderate owner.

Backpacks: Whether you're traveling in black bear or grizzly country, don't make the mistake of getting separated from your backpack. In places like Yosemite, some black bears have learned that packs often contain food. If you leave your backpack and walk off to take a photograph, a bear might get into your pack while you're gone. No matter where you are, don't give bears a chance to investigate your food and gear. In addition to the risk of losing your own food and gear, your mistake could corrupt a bear and teach it to investigate the gear of other people in the future. Carry your gear with you or stash it as carefully as you would when you set up camp for the night.

Islands: Bears are excellent swimmers, so whether you're kayaking along the coast of British Columbia or paddling in the Boundary Waters Canoe Area, be aware that, while small islands often have lower bear densities than other locations, they're not necessarily safe havens from bears.

GRIZZLY TIPS

> If the fear of traveling in bear country is overpowering perhaps it is best that you travel on trails where there is little chance of encountering a bear. Ask at a ranger station or visitor center for their recommendations. There are numerous trails to visit in the Greater Yellowstone ecosystem. You have the luxury of choosing where to travel; the grizzly, due to limited habitat, does not.
> —*Yellowstone National Park,* Beyond Road's End

Grizzlies hate surprises. Yellowstone Park wildlife biologist Kerry Gunther reviewed bear-related injuries in the park from 1980 to 1994 and found that eighteen of twenty-one injuries resulted from people surprising a grizzly in close quarters.[28] Don't surprise grizzlies and don't let them surprise you. I can't emphasize strongly enough that distance is a critical element when you're dealing with grizzlies. You don't want to step into a grizzly's magic circle.

During a serious charge, a bear will come at you on all fours with its ears back, head low, and mouth open. Stand your ground! (Larry Aumiller)

BE AWARE

Fortunately, grizzlies and humans tend to avoid each other. If you pay attention to what you're doing, you will frequently notice grizzlies before they're aware of you. And grizzlies are aware of their surroundings enough that they often detect people before we're close enough to pose a threat. Contrary to popular belief, grizzlies don't want trouble. That's really what the statistics from Yellowstone tell us. Between 1980 and 1994, there were more than 600,000 visitor-use nights in the backcountry and thousands of people went for day hikes, yet there were only twenty-one grizzly bear–related injuries. Grizzlies don't want trouble with you or with other bears—they want food. They're experts at avoiding confrontations and fights.

One day at McNeil River, I saw a subadult male who was fishing for salmon on a gravel bar get sandwiched between a female with a spring cub 40 yards upstream and another big bear about 50 or 60 yards downstream. There was a steep bank thickly covered with alder behind the bears. Everything was fine until mama bear and her cub started walking toward the subadult's fishing hole. He watched them for a moment and then took a look downstream. Whoops. Trouble in every direction. The female and cub kept coming the subadult's way, so he clambered up the embankment. As mama bear walked downstream with her cub, I saw movement in the alders that showed the subadult was headed in the opposite direction. Mama bear stopped at his old fishing hole; moments later, the brush parted and he emerged at her former fishing hole. That's a typical bear encounter.

Just as grizzlies try to avoid confrontations with each other, they generally try to avoid us. Humans rely primarily on sight to detect grizzlies from a safe distance. Grizzlies depend on their nose but have good vision and hearing, too.

You'll often read that it's important to keep the wind at your back so bears can smell you coming, but that's usually not possible when you're hiking on a trail. You go where the trail leads regardless of wind direction. You should still pay attention to the wind, however. You need to be extra careful when the wind is in your face because then bears are less likely to hear you and won't be able to smell you. If the wind is blowing in the wrong direction, it negates the bear's best early warning system.

The fact that humans tend to believe what they see while bears have more faith in their sense of smell probably explains why we place so much emphasis on making noise in bear country. We can't "see" our smell drifting toward a bear, so we don't believe bears can smell us. If they can't smell us and we can't see them, the only way to inform them of our whereabouts is to make noise.

A lot of noise. So people wear bear bells. They travel in large groups and talk, talk, talk. They have nonstop conversations that last for hours. They yodel or sing opera or blast boat horns. Some people insist that metallic sounds are the best way to alert bears of your presence because there are no metallic sounds in nature.

On the maze of trails that lace parks like Yellowstone and Jasper, there are so many people hiking through grizzly country that the amount of noise you make raises ethical and esthetic concerns. All the commotion displaces grizzlies from their preferred habitat. It ruins the tranquillity for other hikers who came to the backcountry to escape the city's mechanical sounds. It disturbs bison, mountain goats, trumpeter swans, and other wildlife. Those critters don't have anywhere else to go. You do. If you're so nervous about grizzly bears that you have to make an excessive amount of noise, why not hike someplace where there are no grizzly bears?

Of course, the key word here is "excessive." What's excessive? Everyone has their own definition. You'll have to decide for yourself when you're afield.

Personally, I clap my hands or give a loud "hey bear" when necessary. I'd hike in a Scottish kilt and cowboy boots before I wore bear bells or walked with a group of people that talked nonstop for 8 hours straight. What would you talk about? The Internet? The World Series? Cosmetics? If you're walking through Jasper National Park's backcountry talking and thinking about politics, perhaps you should reconsider your whole approach to the wilderness.

My philosophy is to leave the urban world behind and focus outward. I strive to see or hear grizzlies before they're aware of me. I pay attention. I think about where I am and what I'm doing. Your brain is your best defense in bear country; I don't believe it's possible for your brain to simultaneously tune out the steady ring, ring, ringing of bear bells, talk about what you're going to have for dinner, *and* focus on your surroundings.

My friend Yellowstone winterkeeper Steve Fuller says he often notices trainlines of noisy hikers while riding his horse in the backcountry, but they're not always aware of him. They're not paying attention. "Physically," says Fuller, "they've escaped the city and left behind the walls of their apartments and automobiles. But not mentally. They're alienated from the environment."

The kinds of hikers who don't spot a man sitting on a 1,000-pound horse aren't likely to see a 400-pound bear that's only 3 feet tall at the shoulders. They're operating on four dubious assumptions. One, it's the bear's responsibility to hear them coming. By making noise they've done their part; the rest is up to the bear. Two, bears *will* hear them coming. Three, a bear will leave when it hears them approaching. Four, it's all right to drive grizzlies away from their food and preferred habitat—not to mention disturbing other wildlife and hikers.

Instead of bludgeoning your way through the woods like Attila the Hiker, why not think of yourself as a guest in grizzly country, a polite visitor who doesn't want to disturb his or her hosts more than necessary? Make an effort to see or hear grizzlies before they notice you. Just as you can see better at night if you close your eyes tightly for a minute and then look around, you'll hear a lot better in the wilds if you begin your hike by getting away from the trailhead and then just sitting quietly for a few minutes and listening. Remember that urban noise is more than the sound of jets overhead and blaring car horns; the worries about work and relationships and other errant thoughts that clutter your brain are just noise and static that interfere with your ability to focus on the natural world you're about to enter. Try to clear your head before you enter bear country.

Bears can be noisy as they flip over rocks, rip apart decaying trees, and bash through thick brush. It's possible to hear grizzlies before you see them—if you aren't making a lot of racket yourself.

Don't make the mistake of expecting grizzlies to notice you. Sometimes bears are totally engrossed with activities like feeding or playing.

Sometimes they can't hear you approaching because of the wind or the noise of a stream. Sometimes bears have their head up their posterior. I doubt if they're thinking about politics, but they're so preoccupied with some bearish thought they won't notice you.

I'm not saying you shouldn't make noise in grizzly country. There are times when it's necessary and appropriate. I just think you need to balance your concern for personal safety with your responsibilities to others.

Because my goal is to spot bears before they're aware of me, I consider binoculars an indispensable tool in grizzly country. I use them frequently. They help you spot bears when they're still a safe distance away. Binoculars allow you to see into dense timber and thick brush. Sometimes you'll hear a branch snap or notice a flash of movement. You might just see an unusual shape. With binoculars, you can pick out a patch of fur you'd miss with the naked eye. You watch and suddenly an elk will materialize. Or a grizzly.

When I worked as a fire lookout in northwest Montana, I learned to scan ridgelines for smoke. If there was a fire on a mountainside facing me, it was pretty obvious. If there was a fire on the other side of a ridge, all I'd see was smoke on the horizon. Scan the horizon in grizzly country. Check out the ridgelines and hilltops because you might see the hump of a grizzly or a halo of backlit hair.

It would be nice if enormous chocolate brown grizzlies always fed in bright green fields of 6-inch-tall sedge so we could easily see them, but it's more common to just see parts of a bear. You see a pair of rounded ears above the sagebrush and that's all. You peer into a patch of krummholtz in an alpine valley and notice the dish-shaped profile of a grizzly's head watching you. It helps to have a strong mental image of the animal. My wife is enchanted with rhinos, and when we're in Africa she inevitably sees them before I do. She's so keyed to rhinos that she easily picks out a rhino's horn in what looks like a tangle of brush and branches to me. Once I see the horn, the whole animal begins to take shape. Similarly, your first glimpse of a grizzly probably won't include the whole bear. It's more common to see part of the animal, one piece of the puzzle, before the whole bear becomes apparent to you.

Don't hike at night. You won't be able to see bears; however, they can see just fine at night. In addition, darkness doesn't interfere with their sense of smell. Bears have all the advantages at night.

When you're on the move during the day, choose your rest stops with care. Kayakers who pull ashore on the point of a peninsula will have a good view up and down the beach where bears might be walking. If you were to go just around the point, a bear could come around the corner and take you by surprise. When you make a rest stop, you need to consider visibility, wind direction, and all the other factors you take into account when selecting a campsite. Always try to rest, camp, or move so you have good visibility in your magic circle.

Travelers in grizzly country should watch and listen for ravens, magpies, coyotes, and other scavengers that could be feeding on the carcass of a moose or some other animal. There might be a grizzly nearby. Use your binoculars to scan at the base of avalanche chutes in the spring. If you notice a carcass while you're several hundred yards away, you can detour around it, but do so with care. Bears don't always camp right on top of the carcass. Sometimes they lay up in dense brush nearby.

Because many people have been injured by grizzlies near a carcass, we're often told grizzlies will "defend" a carcass. I think that's an anthropomorphic, inaccurate way of viewing the situation. We're talking about grizzlies here, not a 325-pound Dallas Cowboy's lineman defending a large pizza. In a paper on bear attacks, Steve French points out that a carcass may anchor a bear to a place for a few days.[29] If that place happens to be near a trail, the odds of people having a surprise encounter with a grizzly rise dramatically. We know that surprising a grizzly at close quarters can provoke an instinctive charge that leads to human injuries. We don't know that a grizzly on a moose carcass watches an approaching person and thinks, "This is my food and there's no way I'm going to let that scrawny little human being have one bite of it."

That's not to say a grizzly won't defend a carcass. A big, mature grizzly won't abandon a carcass when a much smaller grizzly approaches. There's no guarantee a grizzly will leave a carcass because of you, either. But I've had a number of meetings with grizzlies on a carcass, and bears will sometimes abandon a carcass if they smell, hear, or see you coming.

If you stumble upon a carcass (there may be a mound of dirt and branches piled on top of it), you're likely to stop and stare for a moment while your brain struggles to grasp the situation. Then you'll get a clear message: Uh oh. This could be bad.

Don't run. Is the wind in your face or at your back? Take a look around. If you don't see a bear, the terrain and cover will dictate whether you should quietly move forward or back away in the same direction you came from. Chances are that if you came in this way undetected, you can leave the same way.

Another situation when you might inadvertently get close to a grizzly is by approaching a bear resting on a day bed. Grizzlies on day beds tend to be more tolerant of intruders than at other times—but that doesn't mean you want to push your luck. Pay attention if a trail takes you through an area that seems like a likely spot for bears to have day beds. Watch for krummholtz stands in alpine country, willow and alder thickets, dense tangles of timber, and downfall. Bears like moist sites on hot days. A grizzly will often scoop out a shallow dog bed–sized depression at the base of a tree. As a rule of thumb, young bears tend to rest in areas with good visibility such as ridges, bluffs, and sandbars. Mature, dominant bears are more likely to bed down in dense brush. During windy weather, grizzlies spend more time than usual resting in day beds. The wind makes them skittish, as they can't smell or hear as well.

MAKING NOISE

Now let's discuss the topic of noise again, including sounds you shouldn't make. The Interagency Grizzly Bear Committee—which includes representatives from the U.S. Fish and Wildlife Service, U.S. Forest Service, National Park Service, and Montana, Wyoming, and Idaho Fish and Game Departments—publishes a brochure titled *Bear Necessities: How to Avoid Bears,* that urges people to make noise when traveling in grizzly country. "Most bears will avoid people and leave an area when they know people are present. Making noise allows the bear to move away before a confrontation occurs. Talking, singing, whistling, yodeling, or wearing bear bells or other noisemakers will all help to let bears know you are coming."[30]

Whistling? Oldtime Alaskans called marmots "whistlers," and a grizzly will dig a ton of rock and gravel out of a mountainside to get one fat little marmot that gave a warning whistle and then dove into its den. Whistling in alpine bear country to move away grizzlies is like blowing on a predator call to frighten coyotes. If you're going to make noise in grizzly country, you don't want to sound like one of the great bear's prey species.

A lot of people rely on bear bells. Anywhere you find grizzlies, you'll probably find bear bells for sale. The joke about bear bells is, "How can you tell grizzly scat from black bear scat? You'll find bear bells in the grizzly scat."

If you're going to tie bear bells to your pack or your boot laces, be aware that bear bells aren't loud enough to be heard over rushing streams or on windy passes. Wearing bear bells is no guarantee that bears will always hear you coming. You can't rely on bear bells alone. It's probably apparent that I think bear bells are obscene. Still, grizzly bears have definitely learned to associate people with bear bells in some places. When they hear the bells, they know there are people about and this decreases the risk of a surprise encounter.

Clap your hands and give a loud "hey bear" when you're coming to a blind corner on a trail. These are noises you always have with you. You can increase the volume and intensity as needed. They help the bear identify you as a human. If you're hiking on a trail that follows along a noisy stream and thick vegetation limits your visibility, make noise. I make noise when I walk through waist-high patches of cow parsnip and other bear foods. I'm especially concerned about surprise encounters with females with cubs, so I say "hey mama. Hey mama bear." I also travel slowly. I stop and go, stop and go, carefully looking around each time I stop. I listen for bears. I don't just holler my fool head off. I never assume that mama bear will hear me, let alone that she's going to leave because she hears me.

Incidentally, when you first spot a bear, it's best to assume it's a female with cubs. Young bears don't always stick close to their mother, and, because cubs are small, they're tougher to see.

GROUP SIZE

One spring I got into a dangerous situation with a female grizzly and cubs while I was out on a photographic expedition with Doug and Lisa Peacock. We found a female with twins feeding in a meadow. We stashed our packs in a tree and then crept around until the wind was in our face and we were hidden in good cover. Mama bear didn't know we were there, although we were close enough that sometimes when Doug snapped a picture the female's head snapped up at the click of the camera.

Our problems began when Doug ran out of film. He had a new camera and couldn't figure out how to open it to change the film. He is not a patient man. He was sweating and cursing softly while trying to pry the !!#&8!! camera apart with his stubby little paws. The operating manual for his camera was in his pack. While Lisa tried to keep Douglas from roaring in frustration, I went back to the packs for the camera manual. This took me closer to the bears.

I'm sure Doug and Lisa assumed I was keeping my eye on the bears, but I lost sight of them momentarily while I was digging around in the pack. After I found the manual I looked around for the bears. I couldn't see them. I didn't hear anything. Ah, what the heck. I assumed that Doug or Lisa had been glancing up now and then to keep tabs on the bears. We all assumed wrong. Not one of us was paying attention the way we should have been. We were so close to mama bear that when she finally noticed us, she charged.

She swerved away before making contact, but it's still embarrassing to know we foolishly ruined the bears' peaceful day. We endangered ourselves and the bears. Looking back with 20/20 hindsight, we were too close, we should have kept our packs with us, and I should never have gone back toward the bears.

All of us had spent years hiking alone in grizzly country without making such a serious mistake, and I think about this incident whenever I read that you should always hike with a group of people because there's safety in numbers. I don't believe that three dolts are safer in grizzly country than one bear-savvy person.

Statistically, however, solo hikers and pairs of hikers are at greater risk in grizzly country. People in groups of four or more are rarely injured by bears. There has never been injury to a group of six or more. There has never been a fatality in a group of four or more. This safety record stems from three factors. Big groups of people tend to make more noise than smaller groups. Thus, big groups are more likely to alert bears of their presence or drive grizzlies away. Large groups of people are more visible to bears. Grizzlies have a greater chance of seeing (or scenting) you in the distance and then moving away. Last, during an uncomfortably close encounter with people, grizzlies are less likely to conclude a rush or charge at a group of people than an individual or a pair of people.

Traveling with a group also comes into play when you're dealing with young bears that are curious and sometimes test people. A young bear that might approach one person on a beach along the coast of Alaska is far less likely to approach a group of people in the same situation. After years of leading groups of people among large numbers of bears at McNeil River, biologists have noticed that bears are more likely to approach a group of one to five people than a group of six to ten. If you go out alone at McNeil, you can almost count on a visit from a young, tolerant bear.

Steve French points out that it's easy for a group of hikers to get separated while hiking on a trail.[31] One person will forge ahead while another visits the bushes; the next thing you know, your group of six is widely spaced apart. When hiker No. 1 tops a ridge and bumps into a bear, the bear doesn't know that five other people are following. It sees one person, and that changes the dynamics of the encounter. You've lost all the advantages of hiking with a group.

Try not to get overconfident if you're hiking with a big group of friends. There's a tendency for each person to think the other person is taking care of business.

Many trails in grizzly country are unsafe by design. They were constructed decades ago without any consideration for your safety or the welfare of bears. They lead you through berry patches and other food sources for grizzlies. They meander through thick brush beside noisy streams. They follow along the edge of meadows and other natural travel routes for bears. They put you on a collision course with grizzlies. To make matters worse, trails allow people to hike at a fast pace. It's difficult to watch for bears (or other wildlife) while you're marching along at a steady 4 miles an hour. Walking on trails allows your mind to wander when you should be paying attention.

Even in heavily used backcountry areas, it's not safe to assume that trails belong to people and the bears belong somewhere else. In Glacier Park, Montana, for example, some grizzly bears have learned to tolerate people on the popular Highline Trail. They use the Highline Trail both day and night. Despite the sheer number of people on the trail, despite the endless ringing of bear bells, despite the endless prattle of inane conversations, you're far more likely to encounter a grizzly on the Highline Trail than on many other trails in Glacier. While I'm not fond of some trails, I must admit that habituated bears along trails are not often involved in altercations with hikers. Over the years in Yellowstone, a relatively small percentage of off-trail hikers have had as many run-ins with bears as the much greater percentage of people hiking on trails.

Cross-country skiers need to be conscious of bears in late winter/early spring. When I worked as a winterkeeper in Yellowstone, I often saw my first grizzly tracks in March. During the unusually mild winter of 1995–96, winterkeeper Steve Fuller saw grizzly tracks in February. Even in Alaska, there are a few bears on Kodiak Island that never hibernate. No matter where you're going, you should be aware of bear hibernation patterns.

In Yellowstone, bear activity in late winter/early spring often occurs in geyser basins and thermal areas. That's where bears have the best prospects of finding edible vegetation. In addition, there might be winter-killed elk, moose, and buffalo. In Denali National Park, peavines are one of the few foods available to grizzlies in the spring. They commonly grow on broad glacier river bottoms that are popular travel routes for hikers. If you're hiking along a river bottom in the spring, you really need to be on the lookout for grizzlies. Think about what kind of food a bear is most likely to be eating at any given time of year when you travel in grizzly country.

Grizzlies leave behind all sorts of signs. Their digging for roots and bulbs can look like somebody was using a Rototiller in a garden. They excavate large holes to dig out marmots and ground squirrels. Grizzlies roll over logs and flip over rocks to get at ladybugs and other insects. You *will* find grizzly tracks or scat if they're in the area.

I always pick apart bear scat to try and discover what the bruins have been eating. It's more than curiosity about their natural foods. I look carefully for bits of plastic and aluminum that tell me I should be prepared to contend with a food-conditioned bear that's been getting into garbage.

Don't cancel your hike just because you find bear sign. Unless you're looking at a steaming pile of half-digested berries or a quivering salmon carcass with bite marks on it, you'll have difficulty telling how long ago a grizzly was in the area. If it was an hour ago, the bear could easily be 5 miles away. Day-old bear sign in Canada's Waterton National Park might have been left by a grizzly that's now 20 miles away in the United States. The good thing about finding bear sign is it has a way of raising your level of bear consciousness.

Along the coast of British Columbia and Southeast Alaska, kayakers frequently pull ashore for rest stops near areas where both brown and black bears fish for salmon. Freshwater streams filled with spawning fish are an obvious place to watch for bears. It's common to have a shoreline with a strip of beach grass, then a wall of dense alder, and then a towering old-growth spruce forest. The beach grass can be tall enough to conceal either black or grizzly bears, and there are sometimes well-defined game trails just inside the spruce forest. If you're going to poke your head into the forest, you'll be momentarily disorientated and have trouble seeing because even on a typically overcast day along the coast, it's much brighter on the water and the beach than inside the cathedral-like forest. Give yourself a minute to adjust to your new surroundings before plunging into the forest.

Give grizzlies the right-of-way on trails or natural travel routes like beaches. That might seem self-evident, but there have been cases where hikers have provoked bears that weren't even aware of them. They shout and wave their arms over their head in an effort to frighten the bear away from the trail. Instead, the bear charges or advances toward them (usually just continuing along the trail). I think the problem stems from the overemphasis on making noise in grizzly country. Some people have blind faith in the idea that grizzlies will automatically run the other way if they hear you coming. That's not always true. In addition, some bear literature gives the impression that grizzlies understand trails are for humans during the day. Sorry, that's not true either. Grizzlies might habituate to people on trails or avoid trails, but they do not have any respect for proprietary rights you might feel for human trails.

BEAR AVOIDANCE OF HUMANS

Most bears will avoid people and leave an area when they know people are present.

—*Interagency Grizzly Bear Committee,*
Grizzly Country, Bear Necessities: How to Avoid Bears

Bear literature constantly stresses that grizzlies "normally" avoid people; however, it's important to understand that avoidance occurs at two levels. It *is* normal for bears to avoid people and other bears in the sense that they don't want you inside their magic circle. Beyond that, the degree to which bears "normally" avoid people is debatable.

Nowadays, grizzlies often flee the moment they sense a nearby human. Is this normal? Historical accounts of the first meetings between Europeans and grizzlies no doubt exaggerate the ferocity of grizzlies; nevertheless, it's clear the bears weren't so quick to run away 200 years ago.

Let's not forget that shortly after the Lewis and Clark expedition killed thirty-seven grizzly bears on their journey to the Pacific, we slaughtered millions of buffalo and began trapping and shooting bears to protect dull-witted domestic livestock. As civilization advanced, ranchers introduced bears to the perils of strychnine, 1080, and other deadly poisons. In the 1960s, Alaska state employees—at the bequest of cattle ranchers on Kodiak Island—gunned down the biggest bears on earth from planes. During Alaska's pipeline days, construction workers fed bears dynamite sandwiches and blew their heads off. In less than 200 years, we reduced the grizzly population in the continental United States from at least 50,000 bears to less than 1,000.

We slaughtered grizzlies with the fervor of a Hitler and the perversity of a Marquis de Sade. Little wonder the few surviving grizzlies have a tendency to avoid us. But we can only say bears normally avoid people if we're willing to say our behavior toward grizzlies during the past 200 years was normal. I'd like to think it was an aberration and that in the future we'll have the grace, the generosity of spirit, to accommodate grizzly bears.

We'll come back to this topic in the final chapter, "Grizzly Bear Recovery and Reintroduction"; for now, I'll just say that hikers who insist grizzlies "normally" run away from people give credence to the arguments of hunters who claim you have to kill bears to teach the survivors to "fear man."

Grizzlies don't always flee from humans, so if you spot a bear that's more than 100 yards away and not aware of you, don't immediately draw attention to yourself. Think about your situation. At that distance, you're not a threat to the bear. There's not much chance it's going to look up, see you, and charge because it feels threatened.

Whether you decide to take evasive actions or stay and watch the bear for awhile, you need to ask yourself a few questions. Which way is the wind blowing? Can the bear smell me? Can I slip away unseen when the grizzly drops down into a ravine 150 yards away? If it moves closer, what will I do?

If there's a route that simply allows you to avoid the bear, use it before the bear gets within 100 yards of you. If you can't get away undetected and the bear starts heading in your direction, I suggest that you alert the bear to your presence in a nonthreatening way when it's 100 to 150 yards away. Just clap your hands and say "hey bear." If it seems inevitable that the bear will become aware of you, the farther away from you this occurs, the better. This gives the bear options.

It can leave. It might decide you're not a threat and keep going about its business. It may rush toward you, but, because of the distance, this action is more likely to be prompted by curiosity than fear. It may stop, stand on its hind legs, and try to smell or see you better. It might ignore you and keep feeding or doing whatever it was doing. Because the bear is now aware of you, it may only be pretending to ignore you—so leave. Once the bear is no longer moving toward you and is doing something besides looking at you, quarter away from it until you're a safe distance apart. By not moving directly away, you give the bear a better chance to see that you're a human; you don't give the bear the impression that its presence is the reason you're retreating. You can still keep an eye on the bear, but don't hang around. Don't risk another encounter with a bear you've already agitated once. Clear out of the area.

Bears and Human Recreation

Even if you don't ride mountain bikes and even if you would never think of getting close enough to a bear to photograph it, you'll find in this chapter valuable tips that apply to all travelers in bear country, whatever their recreational pursuits. Here I focus on photography, fishing, and mountain biking.

PHOTOGRAPHY

> I never approach bears.
> —*Tom Walker,* Outdoor Photographer, *1996*

In the same 1996 issue of *Outdoor Photographer* in which Tom Walker emphasized that he never approaches bears, another prominent photographer said, "I never approach bears quickly and directly."[32]

The problem with s-l-o-w-l-y approaching a bear is that every person has his or her own definition of "slow," and I suspect every bear does, too. While a photographer who honestly believes he's slowly creeping toward a bear moves ever closer, the bear could be thinking, "If that fool sprints three more steps in my direction, I'm going to throttle him."

The one and only thing you can be sure of when you approach a bear is that you're going to put the animal on edge because it has no idea what your intentions are. Human behavior is truly unpredictable. The bear doesn't know whether you're friend or foe. One person wants a photograph; the other wants a bearskin to hang on the wall. The quicker you approach a bear, the closer you get, and the more likely you are to enter the bear's magic circle, engage with the animal, and force it into "fight or flight" mode. Putting bears to flight raises ethical issues. Fighting bears bare-handed could put you in a hospital. And when a photographer takes a gun afield for "back-up," instigates a fight with a bear by approaching it, and then kills the bear when it defends itself, well, that sort of conduct brings up serious moral concerns. If you don't approach bears, you're not likely to face any of these dilemmas.

Just as people traveling in bear country are usually more concerned about bumping into a grizzly bear than startling a black bear, the main safety concern of photographers is getting so close to a grizzly bear that they provoke a rush or a charge. The question photographers ask about taking pictures of grizzlies is, How close is too close? The answer is, It depends.

Are you looking at a female with cubs or a solitary animal? Is the bear in heavy cover or is it in open country? Is it feeding in the vicinity of six other bears at a salmon stream on the coast of British Columbia or feasting alone in a subalpine meadow in Montana? Is it a female in estrus who's likely to attract testy male bears? Most important of all, what previous experience has this bear had with humans? Every situation is different, and every bear is an individual. There are hundreds of variables to consider, and some of them are unknowable—How could a photographer in Denali's backcountry know whether the bear she's looking at was eating garbage at a lodge in Kantishna the night before? It's best to leave yourself a big margin for safety.

Denali National Park requires backcountry users to stay a quarter mile (1,320 feet) away from bears. In *Bear Attacks: Their Causes and Avoidance*, Steve Herrero recommends 1,000 feet. At 1,000 feet, it's possible to get pictures of a bear in its natural surroundings if the light is right and you've got a long lens. At 1,000 feet, you're reasonably safe, and you won't cause undue stress or potential harm to the bear.

What if you're visiting a place like Alaska's Arctic National Wildlife Refuge and you spot a bear 330 yards away that's feeding on berries and not aware of you? I'd say get out your binoculars, enjoy watching the bear, and follow Tom Walker's rule: Don't approach the bear.

Do take a look around and ask yourself what you're going to do if the bear comes closer. When are you going to let it know you're there? Will you be able to drop out of sight and move away when the bear is still a safe distance off? Do you have a good route for avoiding the bear? If you're comfortable with the situation, set up your gear and allow the bear to make the next move. This can get very dicey very quickly. One minute the bear is a reasonably safe 150 yards away and blissfully unaware of you; the next minute it's only 75 yards away. Suddenly the wind shifts. The bear scents you, rears up on its hind legs, and looks in your direction. Now what? (Help the bear locate and ID you as a human being with a loud "hey bear." Slowly, not frantically, wave your hands overhead.)

I suspect a lot of people look at full-frame shots of bears in books and magazines and think, "Wow. The photographer must have been really close to that bear."

They probably were fairly close to the bear, but there aren't many places where it's practical or ethical to get close to a bear. Any honest pro-photographer will tell you that over 90 percent of the bear photos you see in various publications were taken from the road in Denali National Park or at bear-viewing areas like McNeil River or the Brooks River falls in Katmai National Park. When there's a female grizzly with a cub hanging around the road at Sable Pass in Denali National Park during the third week in July, the five pro-photographers lucky enough to have a permit to travel on the park road that particular week will take thousands of pictures of those bears. Some of them will appear in national publications. So many pro-photographers visit McNeil River that after twenty-one years as the Alaska Department of Fish and Game's manager at McNeil River Larry Aumiller can flip through an article about bears in *Audubon* or *National Wildlife* magazine and name many of the bears in the photographs. More and more people are shooting pictures of captive bears. A trainer taps the bear on the end of its nose, the bear snarls, and—voilà—you've got a cover photo for a magazine taken from so close-up you can see cavities in the bear's teeth.

If you're trying to photograph bears in the wild, your goal should be to take pictures without having the bear know you're there. This means keeping some distance away, at least initially. In situations when that's not possible, say when a bear that's 200 yards away *is* aware of you, then you could allow the bear to willingly approach you. Sure it might be safe for you to move a little closer, but your safety isn't the only issue. What about the bear? Photos of grizzlies are commonplace, but the great bear is rather scarce in the Lower 48 states. What justification is there for edging closer and closer and possibly causing the bear to leave?

Some people in this situation don't think they drove the bear away because it nonchalantly walks off rather than galloping away in terror. Typical bear behavior. If two bears were in a similar situation, the subordinate animal would simply amble off long before the other bear got close. If a bear that's aware of you moves off in the other direction, you can be almost certain it's reacting to you. Whether it runs away or slowly waddles into the forest, you're probably the reason it's leaving.

For most aspiring bear photographers, taking pictures of a trained bear or visiting a bear-viewing area managed by a state or federal agency is the only way to go. No matter where you go afield in search of bear photographs, follow these guidelines:

1. Check on local regulations governing the proper distance to maintain between yourself and bears. Different places have different rules, and in parks like Katmai there's one set of guidelines for habituated bears at Brooks Camp and another set of rules for the rest of the park. Designated bear-viewing areas with habituated bears generally have their own rules and guidelines and visitors must know what they are.

2. Never feed bears, and do not try to attract bears with food or garbage.

3. If you find yourself close to a bear and you see behavior that tells you the bear is nervous (see the chapter "Bear Evolution, Behavior, and Biology"), back off at an appropriate moment and give the bear all the space it wants.

4. If you're photographing grizzlies at a location with trees, try to set up near a climbable tree. Remember, you want to climb the tree when it seems like a dangerous situation might be developing. It's almost impossible to climb to a safe height after a bear has begun a charge.

5. If the bear moves away, don't follow it.

6. Never approach bears.

FISHING

Sometimes when I wade out in a stream while I'm fishing in Alaska, I remember pictures I've seen that show a fisherman in a similar situation except there's a bear on the bank behind him and he's obviously not aware of the bear. Watch that backcast. Glance up and down the stream periodically. Fishing in bear country can be a more thrilling pastime than you bargained for.

Black bears, brown bears, and humans all like fish, and this can bring us in close proximity to each other on noisy rivers and brush-choked streams. The noise and limited visibility make it difficult to detect one another. If you fish in bear country, you need to be bear conscious while walking to fishing sites, when actually fishing, and when camping, cooking, and storing food.

If you keep the fish you catch for a meal, gut and clean them away from camping areas. Don't bring them back to camp for cleaning, and don't clean them on the shoreline near someone else's camp. Avoid getting fish odors on your gear and clothes. Puncture the fish's air bladder so it doesn't float, and throw the viscera into swift and/or deep water far enough out in a stream or lake so that it doesn't wash ashore. When you're done cooking your fish, properly dispose of any fish remains (cooked or otherwise) in the water.

Curious bears might check out any canoe or kayak they find on a shoreline; if that canoe or kayak smells or tastes like fish, you could find yourself patching your boat. Because fish have such a strong odor, you need to be fastidious about cleaning yourself and your gear after handling fish.

MOUNTAIN BIKING

> Off-road mountain biking in the grizzly country of the contiguous United States should be avoided. Habitat fragmentation and other serious threats are enough harassment. Besides, we have plenty of trails to ride outside of bear country.
> —*Drew Ross,* Bears *magazine, 1996*

> I have a real problem with mountain bikes, or jet-powered pogo sticks or any other mechanical contrivance in the wilderness. I absolutely reject the idea that you can have a wilderness experience on a bike.
> —*Harvey Manning,* Backpacker *magazine, 1996*

When grizzlies were classified as a threatened species under the Endangered Species Act in 1975, hunters, horsemen, and other "traditional" users of grizzly country outnumbered backpackers by a wide margin. Imagine the outcry if the hunters and horsemen had said "backpacking in the grizzly country of the contiguous United States should be avoided. Habitat fragmentation and other serious threats are enough harassment. Besides, you have plenty of trails to hike on outside of bear country."

Maybe it's not a good idea to make land management policies based on the argument that "we were here first." But in a 1996 article titled "Some Basic Truths of Mountain Biking," the *San Francisco Examiner*'s Tom Stienstra inadvertently hit on several persuasive arguments for not riding mountain bikes in grizzly bear country, especially in the grizzly's few remaining strongholds in the Lower 48 states. Stienstra, a newcomer to the sport of mountain biking, mentioned, "It's quiet. Bikes are perfect for riding obscure dirt roads in national forests. Since bikes are quiet and fast, you can see a lot of wildlife, especially deer, because you are upon them before they have a chance to react."[33]

When you come upon grizzly bears before they have a chance to react, you have violated one of the cardinal rules of safe travel in grizzly country and placed yourself in a dangerous situation. "The increase in mountain biking and the temper of a surprised grizzly," noted *Bears* magazine, "sounds as volatile a mix as gasoline and fire."

Indeed, Jasper National Park had fifteen biker–bear incidents between 1987 and 1995, including one man who was clawed and bitten. There have also been incidents and injuries in Banff, Kluane, and Denali National Parks.

To avoid unpleasant encounters, a brochure by the Interagency Grizzly Bear Committee and Wyoming Department of Fish and Game gives people three standard warnings. First, check on local regulations to make sure mountain bikes are allowed on the trail or road you plan to use. Second, travel in a group. Last, "Don't surprise bears—Be especially cautious when traveling fast downhill on a trail with blind curves. Slow down and make noise before rounding such bends."[34]

Some people put bear bells on their handlebar or saddle so they constantly clang along bumpy roads and trails. As I discuss in the chapter "Camping and Travel Tips," making noise raises ethical and esthetic considerations. You drive away bears and other wildlife, and you drive other people nuts. Harvey Manning, author of numerous hiking guides, recently said, "[I]t's impossible to be nice when I'm driven off a trail by a pack of yipping, chattering youth dressed in their sister's underwear."[35] His comment infuriated mountain bikers in Washington State, but I believe Manning expressed how bears feel about having mountain bikers zoom through their backyard.

The idea of slowing down seems anathema to the sport of mountain biking. In "Some Basic Truths of Mountain Biking," Tom Stienstra wrote, "It's nothing like hiking. Hiking provides a lot of serenity and quiet, still moments. Biking is fast and challenging, with the whoosh of air in your ears. There's excitement, but it comes at the cost of intimacy."

Cross-country skiing on machine-groomed trails—slot-car skiing— is fast and challenging, too. It's exciting. It's a wonderful sport, but when certain rangers in Yellowstone began setting machine-groomed trails in grizzly country in the early 1980s, I protested. The groomed trails for slot-car skiers invaded some of the best spring habitat available to grizzlies.

People were racing through an area where bears could find winter-killed elk and succulent spring vegetation. Was slot-car skiing an appropriate sports activity in a critically important place for grizzly bears? I didn't think so. Slot-car skiing has more in common with sports like basketball or soccer than it does backpacking. The sport of slot-car skiing emphasized speed and technique—the setting was secondary. Well, the setting wasn't secondary to grizzly bears. Slot-car skiing in critical spring grizzly bear habitat struck me as frivolous. Mountain biking in the grizzly's few remaining strongholds in the Lower 48 states is like playing a ping-pong tournament in the ancient cliff dwellings at Colorado's Mesa Verde National Park.

Bears stand on their hind legs so they can see, hear, and smell better. They lunge forward a bit as they drop to the ground, which is often misinterpreted as a charge. Sometimes bears circle downwind to confirm with their nose what they have seen with their eyes. (Larry Aumiller)

Close Encounters

> Most bear charges are a bluff; the bear will often stop short and amble off. If it charges, however, don't move. When contact is imminent, drop down and play dead. Put your hands behind your neck, pull your legs up to your chest, and think of Jesus.
> —*David Stanley,* Alaska–Yukon Handbook, *1985*

STAND YOUR GROUND

Here's the best all-around rule for handling close encounters with bears: If a bear is approaching you, stand your ground. That sounds macho, but I've "frozen in fear" and it's as effective as puffing your chest out and daring a bear to take one step closer.

Whether you're facing a charging grizzly or a bold black bear entering your campsite, stand your ground. In certain situations with certain types of bears, you can do more than just stand your ground, but standing your ground won't make a bad situation worse. Running probably will. Running is likely to elicit a chase response. Trying to climb a tree will probably elicit a chase too. Slowly backing away from a bear during the first few moments of an encounter is usually a bad move that will encourage a curious or predatory bear to keep pressing forward. Stand your ground. In this way, you signal the bear of your intentions.

In essence, once a bear that's 40 yards away charges you and then stops 15 yards away, you're involved in an intricate dance—the problem is that neither of you knows exactly how to lead or follow. You're both dancing impaired. When you reach a point where each of you has a choice of three moves to make, you both might step in the wrong direction and bump into each other or stomp your partner's toes.

The complexity of bear encounters makes me leery of assertions about what a bear is telling you with its body language when it turns broadside or stares intently at you or clacks its teeth. Bear encounters are not that simplistic. Biologist Polly Hessing cautions, "[B]ears may give and respond to subtle postural clues; we might miss or misinterpret these clues. I don't think that bears posture to show their size as a threat to us—I think it's part of trying to diminish the stress engendered by the situation."[36]

After twenty-one years of watching bear–bear interactions at McNeil River, Alaska Department of Fish and Game biologist Larry Aumiller says, "[B]ears will look intently at you for a variety of reasons, but I've never felt that it was more than gaining visual information. Some bears who receive this visual inspection from another bear will become uneasy and move away. I've never felt the actual act of looking or staring at a bear conveyed any message except in the subtlest of interactions."[37]

Aumiller adds, "Broadside orientation of one bear as a signal to another is a widely held 'truth' that, based on my personal experience, is probably untrue. Frontal orientation is the most aggressive and dominating body position."

During a close encounter with a bear, you can forget about subtle body language and focus on one point: Is the bear advancing toward you? When you have a close encounter with a bear, remember that the bear might be a little nervous, too. Huffing and a bit of foam around the bear's lips are signs of stress, not signals from the bear warning that it's about to attack. Don't assume the bear wants to kill you. A curious bear is just interested in checking you out, and even a female with cubs only wants to protect her youngsters. She might decide to threaten you or render you harmless, but she's most likely to protect her cubs by simply moving away from you.

If a bear attacks you—physically touches you—then you have two alternatives: Fight back or play dead. Your response depends on the situation.

If a black bear or grizzly bear enters your tent at night, assume the bear is in a predatory mode and fight back by any means available. People have killed bears with little pocket knives and bonked them on the head with rocks. Hit the bear with your boots. Punch it in the nose. Fight back as if your life depends on it—because it probably does. Some people keep pepper spray in their tent just for this particular occasion. You'd better hope it deters the bear for a while, because you will be incapacitated after spraying inside your tent.

Even if a bear pulls your companion out of a tent, it's not too late to save him or her. Steve French, in his paper on bear attacks (which was written for medical professionals and might make you a little queasy), notes, "Predatory grizzly and black bears rarely kill their victims before consuming them. After dragging them away from camp usually less than a few hundred feet, they concentrate their efforts towards soft tissue or visceral consumption and the victims frequently remain alive for an hour or more. Therefore, a quick, aggressive, and unified response by companions can potentially save the victim's life. Approaching a predatory bear in the dark while it is trying to feed on a human victim is certainly not without risk but is probably the victim's only chance for survival. This action has been successful on several occasions."[38]

In places like Yosemite and the Boundary Waters Canoe Area, it's common for food-habituated black bears to enter campsites. You want to dominate food-conditioned bears (or curious bears); when one walks into your backcountry campsite, bang pots and pans. Clap your hands. Shout at it. Throw things toward it. The closer the bear gets, the more you need to increase the level of your response. The more people the better, although you should be careful not to surround a bear.

Yosemite Park bear literature used to advise people to throw "rocks at" black bears entering camp until a troop of Boy Scouts stoned a bear to death in 1996. (One of the leaders brained the bear with a fist-sized rock.) Now the Park Service tells people to throw small rocks *toward* the bear, not at it.[39] Use something the size of a golf ball or smaller.

The further a bear gets into your camp, the more difficult it will be to drive it out. The sooner you take aggressive actions, the better the chances of forcing the bear to leave. If the bear is already into your food when you first see it, leave it alone. If it gets into your food despite the commotion you make, leave it alone. The only exception to this rule might be a situation in a remote part of Canada or Alaska where the loss of your food could mean weeks of hunger. If you bother a bear that has your food, you might end up with a few bites and scratches. In almost all circumstances, the best thing to do is leave the bear alone and come back after the bear is gone to clean up.

Behaviorally, it can be difficult to distinguish a bear in a predatory mode from a curious or food-conditioned bear. One difference with black bears is that a food-conditioned bear may make threat displays to get you out of the way. Predatory bears don't threaten or vocalize. There's no huffing or blowing, no rushing two steps toward you and slapping the ground. Predatory bears are intensely interested in their victim. They may try to circle behind you, but they keep pressing, keep bearing in. If a black bear seems to be stalking you, keep an eye on it and don't let it circle behind you. Always face the animal. The same aggressive actions that usually drive away a curious or food-conditioned bear entering your camp are likely to rout a predatory bear too. The all-purpose rule for dealing with any black bear that enters your camp is to use mild aggression to drive it away.

If you're in a place like Glacier or Waterton and you don't know whether the bear entering your camp is a black bear or grizzly bear, you should face the bear and stand your ground to see what happens. If it keeps advancing and you lose your nerve, slowly back away and see whether it goes for your tent and/or food or keeps moving toward you. If it follows you, stand your ground and prepare to defend yourself.

DON'T RUN—DON'T RETREAT—DON'T CLIMB TREES

> Don't run—a grizzly can easily outrun the world's fastest human. Running triggers attacks. If the bear charges your first option is to remain standing. The bear may "bluff charge" or run past you.
> —*Flathead National Forest, Montana Department of Fish, Wildlife and Parks*, Living with Grizzlies

It's common for the same bear literature that says "don't run" from a grizzly to claim that grizzlies make "bluff charges." Are the bears really bluffing? This implies that a bear spots a forester picking berries and consciously decides—before charging—to race within 12 feet of the forester and then stop. "Ha, ha. I was just bluffing."

Is this actually what happens? If it's true, then the response of the forester to the charging bear is irrelevant. He could run like hell and it wouldn't matter; after all, the bear is only bluffing.

When you startle a grizzly at close range and it charges, I don't believe the bear is bluffing. These charges are real and, to some degree, your actions determine the outcome of the encounter. Even when a curious subadult grizzly makes just a half-hearted hop-charge toward you, if you take a couple of quick steps back or break and run, your action changes the dynamics of the encounter and the bear may keep coming at you. People who run are far more likely to get knocked down than people who stand their ground.

I don't think black bears that charge people intend to make contact, nor do I think that "bluffing" is the right word to describe their actions. These charges are formalized behavior indicating distress of some kind—not specific to a cause. It's similar to a bear trying to pull a person from a tree, just as it tries to pull a black bear from a tree.

Tree-climbing after a bear charges you is likely to make a bad situation worse. Bears usually get to the tree before people are out of reach and drag them out of the tree by the foot. Two people have been killed in such a fall. After they hit the ground, the bears left the scene. If you don't notice a bear until it's charging, it's too late for tree-climbing. Don't run. If you simply stand your ground, your action will help the bear make the right decision—which is to not make contact. In essence, your body language tells the bear, "Touch me and it will cost you."

You need to make good decisions when you have a surprise encounter with a bear. After that initial moment when you realize there's a bear nearby that seems to be aware of you, make sure it has positively identified you as a human. It might not have a clear take on what you are—so never try to hide. Hiding could draw the bear closer to identify you. Don't yell loudly but do talk to the bear so it hears a human voice. Don't make any quick movements. Slowly, very slowly, step away from trees, rocks, or brush that block the bear's view of you. Help the bear see you. You want it to know you're human.

If it charges, stand your ground. It might swerve at the last second and run by you. If a charging bear stops a few feet short of you and you're having a stand-off, keep still. Any movement could trigger an attack. Any bear in your place would stare at the ground and watch the other bear out of the corner of its eye. If you're feeling nervous, talk to the bear. Use a nice, quiet tone of voice. The right words will come easily. I believe that what you say unconsciously affects your body language. Your words and body language will signal appeasement, yet the fact that you're standing there indicates a willingness to fight. Perfect. After the bear leaves, you change your underpants and finish your hike. When you get home, you're free to embellish the story any way you like: "No, I wasn't scared. It was just a puny subadult. I stared at him and said, 'Get off my trail you little punk.'"

What if you develop an uncontrollable urge to retreat during one of these standoffs? Bad move. Although it's an understandable desire on your part, it's the wrong move in terms of bear behavior. If you do retreat, don't move fast and don't move while the bear is actually approaching you. Make your move when the bear is stationary. Quarter away at an oblique angle. Maintain occasional eye contact with the bear.

PLAYING DEAD

Whether you are charged by a bear or come upon a bear at close range, never play dead until the bear attacks you. Wait for it to make contact. There have been numerous instances where people flopped down and played dead

When you play dead by curling up in the traditional cannonball position, you have a high center of gravity and that could be dangerous. Battling bears will give their opponents a hard shove—almost a punch—that would easily topple a person, and once you move the bear is likely to intensify its attack. (John Marshall)

when a bear was 10 or 20 yards away; the bear then came over to investigate and inadvertently injured them.

While it's most common for startled grizzlies to charge people, there have been a few cases where people surprised a female black bear with cubs at close range and she charged and attacked. This is the one and only occasion when you should play dead during a black bear attack. You could assume she's protecting her cubs rather than launching a predatory attack. Never play dead with a black bear unless you're 100 percent certain you startled a female with cubs. If the attack persists more than a minute or so, it's time to fight back. In any other situation with a black bear attack, fight back immediately.

In places like Glacier or Waterton Park, it's possible that a bear could come bursting out of the brush and attack you before you have any idea of

If you play dead by lying face down, hands crossed behind your neck, elbows tucked tight along your face, and legs slightly apart, you have a low center of gravity and three balance points. A bear would have to work a bit to flip you over. (John Marshall)

whether it was a black bear or a grizzly, a solitary bear or a female with cubs. Because it's incredibly rare for black bears to charge people and attack them, I'd assume I had startled a grizzly and play dead. A startled grizzly—a grizzly acting defensively—generally does not cause serious injuries if you play dead. Neither does a female black bear with cubs that has been surprised. But if you fight back, the severity of your injuries will usually be worse. If the bear worked me over for more than a minute or so, I'd reconsider the situation. Whether the attacker was a startled grizzly or a black bear that had predation on its mind from the beginning, when an attack lasts too long and it seems the bear has lost its initial fury and settled down to eat, playing dead isn't going to save your life. You have to fight back.

When a bear fights or wrestles, it directs most bites and blows to its opponent's head, so you want to protect your head if you're attacked. It's best to lie face down on the ground with your legs slightly spread apart, interlock your hands behind your head, and tuck your elbows tight against the side of your head. You'll have a low center of gravity and a bear will have to flip you over to get at your face and head. A second technique, one you might instinctively use, is to curl up in a ball with your hands behind your head and your legs curled up beneath your chest. The problem with this technique is that balls roll.

Don't get up right away when the bear leaves. Sometimes they wait and watch; any movement could trigger another attack. As Steve French dryly notes in his paper on bear attacks, "Victims who are attacked from a close encounter situation and who immediately protect themselves and do not try to resist typically receive outpatient injuries. However, those who try to get up and leave after the initial attack but before the bear leaves the area typically receive much more severe injuries during a second attack, requiring multiple surgical procedures resulting in permanent cosmetic and/or functional disabilities."[40]

French also notes that if you try to fend off a bear with your hand, forearm, or arm, "bears can readily cause significant neurovascular injuries to these structures."

If you're with a group of people and a bear charges, the most active person in the group is the one most likely to get nailed.

Guns and Pepper Spray

GUNS

When people take firearms afield, it's usually because they're afraid of grizzlies. Before you take your trusty 30-30 off the fireplace mantle and strike off for grizzly country, here are a few points to consider. You're not likely to be charged by a grizzly unless you startle a bear at 60 yards or less. A grizzly can cover 60 yards in 4 to 5 seconds. It will be hurtling toward you at 30 or more miles per hour. Your target area is only about 12 square inches. For bear defense, the U.S. Fish and Wildlife Service in Alaska and the Department of Renewable Resources for Canada's Northwest Territories recommend a minimum of a 12-gauge 3-inch Magnum shotgun firing 1-ounce slugs or a 30-06 with a 200-grain bullet.[41] (The Fish and Wildlife Service does *not* authorize the use of buck shot for its personnel.) Professional hunting guides in Alaska usually rely on a .375 H&H Magnum shooting 300-grain bullets. A .375 H&H magnum has about half again the power of a 30-06 and makes Dirty Harry's famous .44 Magnum look like a squirt gun.

When you take all these factors into consideration, it's clear there's no sense taking a gun afield unless you're proficient with it. Very proficient. In order to "qualify" to carry a gun afield in Alaska, U.S. Forest Service employees using a .375 H&H Magnum must put nine shots (three sets of three) in a 12-inch circle at a range of 15 to 40 yards in 10 seconds or less.[42] That's a reasonable standard for beginners that can be met after a weekend of training—just remember that shooting paper targets is one thing and shooting charging grizzlies is an altogether different matter.

Things happen fast when grizzlies are charging. If you honestly expect to drop a charging bear with a firearm, your actions have to be instinctual. And before you go afield with a weapon, you need to decide when you're going to shoot. You have to mentally draw a line in the sand at whatever distance you're comfortable with. Bear in mind that if you just stand your ground when a grizzly charges, it most likely will break off its charge at a distances of 5 to 25 yards. People with firearms have wounded or killed bears that would have stopped if someone had just aimed a hiking staff at the bear and said "Bang."

Most bear experts draw the line at 10 to 15 yards or less. You need to have a set distance in mind, and the instant there's a close encounter with a bear, you have to pick a rock or bush 10 to 15 yards away and prepare to shoot when the bear reaches that point. People who don't draw a line in the sand are more prone than others to freeze when they face a charging bear. They're mesmerized by the bear and don't shoot until the last second. Sometimes it's too late.

Although a few people have managed to kill a bear with a pistol, more animals have only been wounded by these underpowered and difficult-to-master weapons. Wounding a bear at close range can change the dynamics of an encounter from an agitated bear defending itself to an angry bear attacking you. Pistols and pepper spray have about the same effective range. Most people would have a lot better chance of hitting the bear with pepper spray. Pepper spray would stop the bear just as often as a .357 or .44 Magnum, and pepper spray doesn't kill or wound bears.

Biologists who process the paperwork for DLPs—bears killed in defense of life and property—note that almost everybody who was forced to kill a bear out of season claims they fired a warning shot but it didn't do any good. Now these folks have every reason to stretch the truth, but firing a warning shot probably just wastes ammo and increases the risk of your gun jamming when you quickly chamber a second round. In particular, short people with short arms have a tendency to "short-stroke" pump action shotguns. Professional hunting guides don't fire warning shots because warning shots almost never change the behavior of a bear.

Carrying firearms can give you the peace of mind to stand your ground during an encounter. You might save your life without pulling the trigger. You'll have to fight against overconfidence; don't go anywhere or do anything you wouldn't consider doing if you were unarmed.

PEPPER SPRAY

> The spray is better than nothing, but I don't want to be in a
> situation where I have to use it.
> —*Chuck Jonkel,* Field & Stream, *1987*

Chuck Jonkel is a biologist who helped develop pepper spray during the early 1980s. Although Jonkel found that pepper spray effectively deterred both grizzly and black bears under laboratory conditions, people wondered whether it would work in real-life situations. Most of all, people wondered whether it would stop a charging grizzly bear.

Pepper spray is made from super-hot ground-up peppers (oleoresin capsicum) in a pressurized container. Cans of pepper spray usually weigh around a pound and are roughly 2 inches in diameter and 8 to 9 inches tall; they're much larger than the little keychain or purse-size canisters of mace. You can't take your pepper spray on a plane; you'll be stopped at airport security and your pepper spray will be confiscated. It's also illegal to put pepper spray in your checked baggage. Always warn bush pilots with small planes that you have pepper spray. They can attach it to the wing strut on a wheeled plane or put it in the floats of a float plane. These precautions are necessary because if a can of pepper spray goes off in a small plane, down you go.

Just as there would be trouble if a can of pepper spray went off in a plane, an accidental discharge in your vehicle could be disastrous. At the very least, carry pepper spray in a double layer of resealable plastic bags. At military surplus stores, you can get metal ammo boxes for 7.62 NATO cartridges that can hold three or four cans of pepper spray. They're durable and have an air-tight rubber seal. There are also 60- and 81-mm mortar shell plastic containers available that can hold three cans of pepper spray.

Don't leave pepper spray on the dashboard of your vehicle where it's going to bake in the sun. For long-term storage, the optimum temperature is 50 to 70 degrees Fahrenheit. It's easier on the can's seals if the temperature is constant. Pepper spray has a shelf life of one to three years; there's usually an expiration date marked on the can.

Ontario's Quetico Provincial Park, which is just across the border from Minnesota's Boundary Waters Canoe Area, publishes a guide that says, "To be imported into Canada, Capsaicin Spray must conspicuously state 'that it is for use against dogs and other animals.' The container may not be labeled for use for 'personal protection.'"[43] In the United States, the Environmental Protection Agency prohibits the labels on pepper spray from saying "for use against animals." In other words, it's illegal for Canadians to bring their pepper spray into the United States, and it's illegal for U.S. citizens to take their pepper spray into Canada. If you've got a canoe on top of your vehicle and a trunk full of backpacks and camping gear, customs agents are almost certain to ask whether or not you have pepper spray. You can't take it across the border; be prepared for a stiff fine if you lie and get caught. Pepper spray is illegal altogether in a few states, so inquire locally.

Every can of pepper spray I've seen is equipped with a plastic safety tab that is *not* child-proof. At home and in the field, you must secure pepper spray from children. Pepper spray is burning hot on your skin, and I never want to find out what it feels like to get hit in the eyes. If you get it on your skin, wash it off with soap and either cool water or milk. If possible, wash your face with a nontearing soap or something like baby shampoo. For pepper spray in your eyes, flush them with copious amounts of water. People who wear contacts will no doubt remove them immediately. Due to the porosity of contact lenses, you'll probably never wear that particular pair again. Try cleaning them with an appropriate lens-cleaning solution, but they may sting when you put them back in. You should check with your optometrist.

If you're going to buy pepper spray, get two cans—one to test-fire, and one for later use. If you're experienced with firearms, the first time you pick up a can of pepper spray and aim it, you're likely to point the nozzle at your face. After you figure out which way to aim it and test fire the stuff, you'll probably be surprised at the range. It really doesn't go far. You might also be surprised at the loud hissing noise the can makes and the bright-colored spray. Better to find out about these things during a test in an abandoned woodlot than to startle yourself when a bear is charging you. Make sure you fire downwind. The $30–40 you pay to spray a can that's empty in a few seconds might seem like a lot of money, but you're likely to spend that much on beer and pizza after a week-long hike. It would be penny-wise and pound

Under ideal conditions—no wind or rain—pepper spray only has a range of 18 to 30 feet. Use your head and it's not likely you'll need to use pepper spray. (John Marshall)

foolish to rely on a tool you've never used before to stop a charging grizzly.

Pepper spray fires out in a foggy mist like insect spray. Depending on the manufacturer, it has a maximum range of 18 to 30 feet. One manufacturer cautions that "the most effective range to stop an attack is half the maximum range." In a 10-mile-per-hour crosswind, the spray from pepper spray will start drifting sideways at a distance of about 8 feet. In a hard rain, the kind of rain that's common in Southeast Alaska and along the coast of British Columbia, pepper spray doesn't have much range. Although cold weather—temperatures less than 40 degrees Fahrenheit—affects the performance of pepper spray (or any other aerosol product), you can carry it inside your jacket during the day, and put it in your sleeping bag at night.

This brings up one of the problems of relying on pepper spray too much—when you need it the most—when you startle a bear—you may not be able to get to it quick enough. Whenever it's practical, carry your pepper spray in the same place all the time so you know exactly where to reach when there's a crisis. Most pepper spray comes with a nylon hip holster that has a Velcro flap top, and one manufacturer makes a cleverly designed holster that you can fire from a chest harness. Like a quick-draw artist in an old cowboy movie, you should practice releasing your pepper spray from the holster, drawing it to a firing position, and removing the safety tab. Practice again and again until it's automatic. It's easy to lose the little safety clip, so you might want to tie a piece of elastic shock cord to it.

It's a good idea to test-fire every new can of pepper spray with a half-second burst. If your can of pepper spray has been sitting in the basement for a few months, you can do a makeshift pressure test by gently shaking the can. The contents won't slosh around noticeably if the pressure is good. If it feels like you're shaking a can of soup—if you can feel the liquid sloshing around with every shake—the can has probably lost pressure. In addition to checking the pressure, look for leakage from the seals, the actuator, and the edge of the canister.

A 1995 report on the use of pepper spray as a bear deterrent found that spraying curious brown bears approaching a camp stopped 20 out of 20 bears initially.[44] Two bears came back for a second look. In cases where brown bears charged or behaved in a threatening manner toward people, pepper spray initially stopped the bear's behavior 15 out of 16 times. Six of the sixteen bears continued to behave aggressively and three bears attacked the sprayers.

Pepper spray was less effective on black bears. When used on curious bears or bears looking for food and garbage, 19 out of 26 bears that were sprayed intially stopped what they were doing. Only 14 out of 26 bears left the area, and 6 of those 16 bears returned. When people sprayed black bears during sudden encounters or possible predatory situations, 4 out of 4 bears initially stopped their behavior. However, the bears did not leave the area in response to being sprayed.

These are all real-life incidents, not controlled tests in a lab. The results of the study are based on a total of 66 verifiable incidents, and the authors of the study caution that this is an extremely small sample size.

Larry Clark, from the Monell Chemical Senses Center, notes that Capsaicin may be effective only on the first hit. If a bear gets a good dose, leaves, and then returns a few minutes later, a second dose might not have much effect. Once saturated, the bear might not feel any pain no matter how much you spray it.[45]

In 1984, a man doing grizzly bear research in Yellowstone Park became something of a pepper spray poster boy when he foiled an attack with pepper spray. He first sprayed the grizzly at a distance of 20 feet and then again at 6 feet. After the bear knocked him down, he sprayed it directly in the face and it left. Several national publications in articles about pepper spray have used this incident to make the point that pepper spray really works.[46]

I'm not sure I agree 100 percent with that conclusion. The researcher involved in this incident was working for the Interagency Grizzly Bear Study's "Bear Disturbance Crew," which was more commonly known as the "suicide squad." Their job was to go into backcountry areas and disturb bears to show how they reacted. This brings me to a point I can't emphasize strongly enough: Just because you have a can of pepper spray, don't go places you wouldn't go otherwise. Don't do things you wouldn't do otherwise. Try to guard against overconfidence. The record clearly shows that pepper spray can be effective for stopping bear attacks and even more so against curious or food-seeking bears. What the record doesn't tell us is how often pepper spray indirectly caused the same attacks.

In a recent phone conversation, Yellowstone Grizzly Foundation Co-Director Steve French told me he's gone through three distinct phases on pepper spray. At first he categorically rejected it. Then he carried it everywhere and found that it made him too cocky. He couldn't control the overconfidence factor. Now he doesn't take pepper spray with him on day-to-day field excursions, but he does keep it handy in camp. French, an articulate man who describes himself as "the son of a Texas truck driver who happens to be a doctor," always reminds people that pepper spray "ain't brains in a can."

Grizzly Bear Recovery and Reintroduction

The Endangered Species Act . . . prohibits activities on federal lands
or by federal agencies that would contribute to population declines.
Under section 7 of the ESA, federal agencies such as the Forest
Service must consult with the U.S. Fish and Wildlife Service prior to
taking any action that may affect a listed species. By law, the FWS
must issue a biological opinion that evaluates the proposed activity.
Where an activity will "jeopardize" a species, the activity must be
modified or forgone.

> —*U.S. Fish and Wildlife Service,*
> Grizzly Bears in the Cabinet/Yaak Ecosystem

The needs of the grizzly bear will be given priority over other
management considerations.

> —*Definition of "Management Situation One"*
> *Grizzly Bear Habitat in the U.S. Fish and Wildlife Service,*
> Grizzly Bear Recovery Plan, *1982*

Today's grizzly bear recovery plans are like yesterday's Indian treaties: We
break every promise except one—we take the land. We take the land and give
it to timber companies and ranchers. We take the land and hand it to hunters and hikers and the ORV crowd. There wasn't enough land for grizzlies
when they were classified as a "threatened species" in 1975, and there's far less
land now. In each of the six official grizzly bear recovery areas—Cabinet–Yaak,
North Cascades, Northern Continental Divide, Selkirk, Selway–Bitterroot,
and Yellowstone—grizzlies are worse off now than in 1975.[47]

Grizzly bear recovery efforts reached a low point in 1995, when a federal district court ruled that the 1993 version of the U.S. Fish and Wildlife
Service's oft-revised Grizzly Bear Recovery Plan was "contrary to law." Judge

Paul Friedman ruled that the plan failed to evaluate the factors that led to the original listing of the grizzly, including habitat destruction. He rejected parts of the plan that failed to address the threat caused to grizzly bear populations by bear–human conflicts resulting from grizzly bear predation on livestock. Most importantly, Judge Friedman noted that the recovery plan did not "access present or threatened destruction, modification, or curtailment of the grizzly bear's habitat or range."

Judges are not biologists. A judge would only rule against a recovery plan that had virtually no scientific merit. Judge Friedman's 1995 ruling tells us the grizzly bear recovery plan is garbage. It's a paid political speech, not a credible scientific document.

The National Academy of Sciences should review the existing body of literature on bear biology. We need a sound, objective, scientific assessment to determine (a) the leading causes of direct and indirect bear mortality, (b) how much habitat grizzlies need, and (c) the best method of determining long-term population trends.

In conjunction with a sound biological analysis on grizzly bears, we need a solid financial analysis on the cost of saving—and destroying—grizzly bear habitat.

According to a 1995 article in the *Kalispell (Montana) Daily Inter Lake,* "The Flathead [National Forest's] timber program ended budget year [19]94 some $2.8 million in the red. . . . In the last 10 years, the Flathead timber program has been in the black only once."[48]

Why should taxpayers subsidize the destruction of grizzly bear habitat? These financial losses occur despite using unorthodox Forest Service accounting procedures that do not bill timber companies for the cost of building or maintaining roads. Since grizzlies were classified as a "threatened species" in 1975, 1,709 miles of logging roads have been built on the Flathead at a cost of about $25,000 a mile. That's a $42,725,000 bill for taxpayers. After accounting for the cost of logging roads and other factors the Forest Service ignores, University of Utah economist Michael Garrity estimated that planned Forest Service logging in the Selway–Bitterroot grizzly bear recovery area will cost taxpayers $137 million between 1997 and 2006.[49] Wouldn't it make more sense to not log the land, save the habitat for grizzlies, other wildlife, and human enjoyment, and save taxpayers $137 million?

Livestock grazing on public lands is heavily subsidized, too. Representative Bruce Vento, D-Minn., a co-sponsor of the Public Resources Deficit Reduction Act of 1995, told the Associated Press that "the federal grazing program loses more than $50 million a year."[50]

In the same article, Rep. George Miller, D-Calif., said the bill would save "up to $850 million annually in government logging operations, partly by halting all timber sales that end up costing more than the revenue they return."

We need a team of independent economists or the Government Accounting Office to review Forest Service bookkeeping methods for timber sales and to check into grazing subsidies. We need to find out exactly how much the public pays ranchers to run cows and sheep on public land in grizzly country.

What follows is my analysis of several key issues concerning the long-term welfare of grizzly bears.

PREMATURE DELISTING

Sportsmen's journals have published a "we need to hunt the grizzly" story about once every year or two. As an example, consider the following "notice," published in *Outdoor Life* in 1980, just five years after grizzlies were listed as a threatened species. It was titled "Yellowstone Grizzly Hunts Foreseen":

> The grizzly bear has been considered a threatened species in most of the Lower 48 states and is protected under the Endangered Species Act. But near Yellowstone National Park, grizzlies are making such a strong comeback that a limited amount of hunting may be permitted after the US Fish and Wildlife Service reviews grizzly status in the area. . . . [W]hen protected bear populations increase the animals invade areas inhabited by humans [and] the bruins also begin to lose their fear of people and become potentially dangerous nuisances to hikers, backpackers and campers. "We've reached the stage," says Montana game official Gene Allen, "where limited, controlled grizzly hunting is becoming a necessity."[51]

When grizzlies are no longer protected by the Endangered Species Act, we can expect every state with grizzlies to declare an open season on the great bear. There would also be a dramatic increase in resource extraction and recreational use. Knowing this, it is critical to give grizzlies as much habitat as possible in order to offset predictably high mortality rates. (Incidentally, a court order ended Montana's grizzly hunting season in the Northern Continental Divide Ecosystem (NCDE) in 1992, and there has not been a significant change in bear behavior or bear–human conflicts.)

LOGGING AND LOGGING ROADS

> Roads probably pose the most imminent threat to grizzly habitat
> today. Any unroaded land represents important and unique
> opportunities. . . . Management should seek to maintain these
> areas as unroaded whenever possible.
>
> *—U.S. Fish and Wildlife Service,*
> *Bear Recovery Plan, September 1993*

Since grizzlies were classified as a threatened species in 1975, the Kootenai
National Forest has built more than 1,600 miles of logging roads and reduced the amount of roadless land in the Cabinet–Yaak from 887,000 acres
to 607,000 acres. What do logging and logging roads on a scale like this
mean to grizzlies? Death. One study in the NCDE found that 63 percent of
all grizzly bear mortality occurred within 0.6 mile of a road, whereas another one (Mattson and Knight, 1991) found that secondary roads in the
Yellowstone region increase the risk of grizzly bear mortality by five times.[52]

This calls for no more logging in roadless grizzly habitat and no more
deficit timber sales. We need prompt development and implementation of
road density standards for all grizzly habitat. We need to eliminate new
roadbuilding in grizzly country that exceeds 0.5 road miles per square mile
of habitat. Money earmarked for deficit timber sales should be used to close
and restore roads where excess road densities occur.

LINKS BETWEEN RECOVERY ZONES

The magnitude of logging allowed by the Forest Service and Fish and Wildlife Service since 1975 has cut off grizzlies in the Cabinet Mountains from
grizzlies in the Yaak. The former Cabinet–Yaak has been severed from the
NCDE and the Selway–Bitterroot recovery zone to the south. Isolated "island populations" are extremely susceptible to local extinction. In terms of
practical results, the Grizzly Bear Recovery Plan has been a grizzly bear
eradication plan. We should target roads for obliteration in order to reestablish links between recovery zones.

ROAD MANAGEMENT PROGRAMS

The Forest Service does a great job of building roads, but a laughable job
of closing them. Numerous investigations by environmental organizations
have proven that road closures are ineffective, and this was confirmed when
the U.S. Fish and Wildlife Service looked at road closure effectiveness in the

Selkirk recovery area in 1994. It found that 80 to 100 percent of the road closures were passable by motorcycles and 40 to 90 percent were passable by larger ORVs. Gates and locks do not suffice for road closures. Roads must be obliterated.

LIVESTOCK AND GRAZING

In 1948, biologist Adolph Murie published a study in the *Journal of Wildlife Management* about grizzly bear predation on livestock on public land south of Yellowstone Park. "A number of grizzlies have been taken off the cattle range over a period of years," wrote Adolph Murie, "but the predation has persisted."[53]

It certainly has. During the summer of 1995, grizzlies took 13 of the 1,600 cattle on the 88,000-acre Blackrock–Spread Creek grazing allotment near Togwotee Pass on the Bridger–Teton Forest Service.[54] Ranchers not only demanded government compensation for the cattle lost; they also claimed that the presence of grizzlies makes cattle so nervous that reproductive rates drop and the cattle don't put on as much weight as they should. Ranchers want financial compensation for these losses, too. They also expect the government to move grizzlies off "their" grazing allotment in Management Situation 1 grizzly habitat. This is the same area where Murie did his study in 1948. Livestock means death for grizzlies (and for wolves, coyotes, and all other predators)—always has, always will. There should not be any livestock grazing allotments in grizzly habitat.

LOCAL VERSUS NATIONAL INTERESTS

In the early 1990s, a proposal to augment a small population of grizzlies in the North Cascades divided Washington's outdoors community. Many people frankly admitted they were afraid of grizzlies; others feared that bringing back the bear might result in trail closures and other restrictions. With strong support from timber and livestock industries, the anti-grizzly side won the battle. The Fish and Wildlife Service shifted funding for grizzly restoration in the Cascades to wolf reintroduction in Idaho. Now people can proudly tell their grandchildren they made the Cascades safe for sheep, cows, and clearcuts.

I don't think we should let Washington residents decide the fate of the grizzly on National Park and National Forest lands any more that we should cave in to the incessant demands of Alaskans to drill for oil in the Arctic National Wildlife Refuge.

The greatest threat to grizzlies everywhere is locals who view bears as a threat to their "traditional" way of life. Loggers, hikers, mountain bikers, ORV users, ranchers, and hunting outfitters all define "traditional" as how they work or play on public lands. Logging is no more traditional than Nintendo or jet-skis. For centuries before ranchers along the Rocky Mountain Front killed all the bears and wolves to make way for sheep and cattle, Blackfeet Indians had a tradition of hunting bison in the same area. Now the Blackfeet's way of life is gone, and the only steady form of employment on the reservation is working at a pencil factory. Why not get rid of domestic livestock on the public's land and bring back the bears and buffalo? Traditional ranchers would no doubt go out of business without traditional government subsidies, but they can always work at the pencil factory. Instead of putting erasers on pencils, the Blackfeet could manage former grazing allotments with an eye toward the future.

U.S. BEAR POPULATIONS THAT SHARE A COMMON BOUNDARY WITH CANADA

We cannot count on bears from Canada moving south across the border to replenish supplies in the United States. One look at an ordinary highway map and you can see that there are towns, highways, and relatively high levels of development all the way from the Cascades east to the Yaak. The B.C. Ministry of Environment, Lands and Parks recently released a map titled "Grizzly Bear Habitat Potential in B.C.: Possible Future Suitability, 2065." Except for a smidgen of land just north of Glacier Park, all land west to the boundary of Washington State would have "reduced grizzly bear populations." All land north of Washington would be "extensively modified urban and rural habitats—extirpated grizzly bear populations."[55]

British Columbia has proposed a number of "protected areas and special management areas" but, with one notable exception, they're so far north of the border they're not "linked" to U.S. grizzly populations. British Columbia does have parks and protected areas just north of the struggling bear population we've abandoned in the North Cascades.

According to a 1996 poll conducted by state and federal wildlife officials in Washington, more than 70 percent of the state's residents want to boost the grizzly bear population in the North Cascades. If wildlife officials truly want a recovery plan to succeed, they could start by being honest with the public about the "costs" of bringing back the great bear. A 1993 booklet called "Grizzly Bear Recovery in the North Cascades" attempts to placate hikers by claiming that "effects on recreation in the North Cascades are expected to be minimal." Sorry, recreational use in the Cascades is far greater than in places like Yellowstone or the NCDE. Hikers don't pose a direct threat to grizzlies—we don't shoot them—but due to illegal hunting and other types of human harassment throughout the Cascades, grizzlies would tend to avoid all people everywhere—including areas heavily used by hikers. That doesn't leave enough habitat for bears. There's so much recreational use in the Cascades I really believe it would be necessary to close some trails, at least on a seasonal basis.

Of course it will also be necessary to curtail commercial logging, comply with sensible food storage regulations, eliminate livestock grazing allotments, etc. Biologists today have the knowledge to look at a map of the Cascades and predict with 90 percent accuracy where conflicts between bears and people will occur. We also know where grizzlies will find food, and when that food will be available. The question is, do grizzlies or people have top priority in these areas? The more we compromise grizzly habitat to accomodate human use, the more agencies must lie or use specious logic to defend habitat degradation, and this is what makes "grizzly bear management" so complex.

Americans have always assumed that Canada has grizzly bears to spare, and will happily give them to us to augment grizzly bear populations in places like the Cascades. Wrong. Canada doesn't have any extra grizzlies, or at least not many. There's no reason why Canada should give the United States grizzlies for foolish experiments. In the early 1990s, we transplanted four grizzlies from British Columbia into Montana's 90,000-acre Cabinet Mountain Wilderness. Those bears were doomed from the start because you can't have more bears than you have bear habitat. If Canada is kind enough to donate more grizzlies, wouldn't it make more sense to transplant them in the Cascades? The 10,000-square-mileNorth Cascades Grizzly Bear Recovery area is bigger than Yellowstone or any other recovery area—and it's adjacent to a part of British Columbia that supports a small population of grizzlies. Transplanting a few bears to the North Cascades would benefit bears on both sides of the border.

BEAR RESEARCH
In the February 1986 *National Geographic,* pioneering bear researcher John Craighead said, "We already know enough about grizzly bear biology to save these bears. No matter what else we learn, we're not going to have grizzlies very long unless we preserve large enough tracts of good wildland habitat.

Too often when a tough political decision in favor of the bear is called for, we put it off by ordering up another research project to—you know—'study the situation.' We could end up studying the grizzly to death."[56]

We don't need more studies about the adverse effects of building roads in grizzly country—we need to obliterate hundreds of miles of logging roads. All too often the goal of research is micromanagement: What's the maximum number of bears we can allow hunters to harvest in a given area without doing long-term harm to the overall population? Instead of giving biologists and bureaucrats carte blanche to do whatever research they want, an independent team of scientists should review proposals for bear research and ask, What's the purpose of this study? How will it help bears?

RECOVERY IN THE SELWAY–BITTERROOT

There is currently a bitter debate between environmentalists about how to recover/reintroduce grizzlies to the Selway–Bitterroot. There's a core wilderness area (Selway–Bitterroot and Frank Church–River of No Return) of about 3.7 million acres of designated wilderness in the Selway–Bitterroot surrounded by another 4 million acres of National Forest and other public lands. Some people favor the "Conservation Biology Alternative," which would selectively obliterate roads on land surrounding the wilderness core to reclaim grizzly habitat and reestablish links to the Cabinet Mountains and beyond. Bears would be fully protected under the Endangered Species Act.

Other people favor the "Community Based Alternative," which would essentially stock grizzlies in designated wilderness areas and leave decisions about bears and land management outside the wilderness in the hands of locals. When I think about what happened to the Cabinet–Yaak during the past twenty years, I'd say that within a few generations the wilderness boundaries of the Community Based Alternative would be marked by clearcuts, just as the boundary between Yellowstone Park and the Targee National Forest is delineated by clearcuts that can be seen by astronauts in outer space. It's not just logging roads that are bad for bears; it's the unsustainable levels of cutting. The core wilderness area would be a large open zoo that needed to be re-stocked with grizzlies periodically.

In contrast, the Conservation Biology Alternative is a visionary plan. It would offer sustainable levels of logging and industry and a reasonable amount of recreation.

If the National Academy of Sciences and the Government Accounting Office carefully analyzed recovery plans for each of the six grizzly bear recovery areas, I'm positive the recommended plan for each area would closely resemble the Conservation Biology Alternative for the Selway–Bitterroot.

I believe the act of restoring a home for the great bear will help restore in us the generosity, reverence, and sense of reciprocity with the earth that make up the foundation of our humanity.

notes

1. Alfred Runte, *Yosemite: The Embattled Wilderness* (Lincoln: University of Nebraska Press, 1990).
2. Alan Carey, "The Charge," in *Field & Stream,* February 1984, 70.
3. Stephen Herrero and Andrew Higgins, "Human–Black Bear Interactions," in *Proceedings of the 5th Western Black Bear Workshop,* ed. Janene Anger and Hal L. Black (Provo, Utah, 1995).
4. Polly Hessing, letter to author, June 30, 1996.
5. National Audubon Society and TBS, coproducers, *Grizzly and Man: Uneasy Truce,* 1989, video.
6. Derek Stonorov, letter to author, June 1996; Derek Stonorov and Allen W. Stokes, "Social Behavior of the Alaska Brown Bear," in *Bears—Their Biology and Management,* n.s., no. 23 (Morges, Switzerland: International Union for the Conservation of Nature and Natural Resources, 1972), 232–42.
7. *Yellowstone Grizzly Journal* 8, no. 3 (Spring 1996).
8. Cited in Ellis Sutton Bacon, "Investigation of Perception and Behavior of the American Black Bear (*Ursus americanus*)" (doctoral dissertation, University of Tennessee, Knoxville, 1973). The original report is by E. Kuckuk, "Tierpsychologische Beobachtungen an zwei jungen braunbaren," *Zeitschrift für Vergleichende Physiologie* 24 (1937): 14–41.
9. Lyle Willmarth quoted by Tom Beck, letter to author, August 16, 1996.
10. Interagency Grizzly Bear Committee, *Bear Us in Mind* (Washington, D.C.: Government Printing Office, 1986).
11. E. Watson, "Grizzlies," *Sports Illustrated* 27, no. 19 (1967): 63–67.
12. "Smelly Socks Attract Grizzly," *Anchorage Daily News,* October 27, 1995.
13. Caroline P. Byrd, "Of Bears and Women: Investigating the Hypothesis That Menstruation Attracts Bears" (master's thesis, University of Montana, Missoula, 1988); U.S. Department of the Interior, National Park Service, Glacier National Park, *Grizzly Bear Attacks at Granite Park and Trout Lake in Glacier National Park, August 13, 1967* (West Glacier, Mont., 1967).

14. U.S. Department of the Interior, *Grizzly Bear Attacks,* 21–22.

15. Bruce S. Cushing, "The Effects of Human Menstrual Odors, Other Scents, and Ringed Seal Vocalizations on the Polar Bear" (master's thesis, University of Montana, Missoula, 1980).

16. C. R. Morey, wilderness specialist, to administrative officer, memorandum, *Backcountry Assignments for Female Employees,* November 13, 1980, Glacier National Park.

17. B. Blacker, L. Tryon, G. Johnson, K. Ahlenslager, L. Williams, M. Eisheid, G. Seeley, P. Lazo, and S. Gill, to acting superintendent, letter, December 15, 1980, Glacier National Park.

18. Hutchison, acting regional director, to regional director, Rocky Mountain Region, memorandum, *Backcountry Assignments for Female Employees,* May 29, 1981.

19. Jean O'Neil, acting superintendent, Glacier National Park, management directive no. 203.4, *Women in the Backcountry,* April 6, 1984.

20. Stephen Herrero, *Bear Attacks: Their Cause and Avoidance* (New York: Lyons & Buford, 1985), 139.

21. Lynn L. Rogers and S. S. Scott, "Reactions of Black Bears to Human Menstrual Odors," *Journal of Wildlife Management* 55, no. 4 (1991): 632–34.

22. Kerry A. Gunther, *Bears and Menstruating Women,* Yellowstone National Park, Information Paper BMO-7, 1995.

23. Byrd, "Of Bears and Women," 17.

24. William B. Cella and Jeffery A. Keay, *Annual Bear Management and Incident Report* (National Park Service, Yosemite National Park, 1980).

25. Denton W. Crocker, *Wilderness Camping* 6, no. 2.

26. Kerry Gunther, personal communication, November 1996.

27. Steve and Marilyn French, "The Predatory Behavior of Grizzly Bears Feeding on Elk Calves in Yellowstone National Park, 1986–1988," study presented at the International Conference on Bear Research and Management, 1990.

28. Kerry Gunther and Hopi Hoekstra, "Bear-Inflicted Human Injuries in Yellowstone, 1980–1994," *Yellowstone Science* 4, no. 1 (Winter, 1996): 2–9.

29. Steven P. French, M.D., section in "Bites and Injuries Inflicted by Mammals," in *Management of Wilderness and Environmental Emergencies,* 3d ed., ed. Paul S. Aeuerbach (St. Louis: C. V. Mosby, 1995).

30. Interagency Grizzly Bear Committee, *Bear Necessities: How to Avoid Bears* (Missoula, Mont., n.d.).

31. Steve French, telephone conversation with author, September 1996.

32. Erwin Bauer, "Big Bears," *Outdoor Photographer,* March 1996, 40–43, 104–5.

33. Tom Stienstra, "Some Basic Truths of Mountain Biking," *San Francisco Examiner,* 1996. Reprint, *Anchorage Daily News,* September 1, 1996.

34. U.S. Fish and Wildlife Service, Wyoming Department of Fish and Game, Interagency Grizzly Bear Committee, *Mountain Biking,* brochure (n.p., n.d.).

35. Harvey Manning, quoted by Peter Potterfield, in "The Warrior Writer," *Backpacker* magazine, August 1996, 56–62.

36. Polly Hessing, letter to author, June 30, 1996.

37. Larry Aumiller, letter to author, June 1996.

38. Steve French, "Bear Attacks." This is the draft version of French's section that later appeared in Auerbach, *Management of Wilderness and Environmental Emergencies.*

39. U.S. Department of the Interior, National Park Service, *The Bears Are Not to Blame,* brochure (Washington, D.C., 1995); Steve Thompson, Yosemite's Resource Management Office, telephone conversation with author, September 1996.

40. Steve French, "Bear Attacks."

41. U.S. Department of the Interior, Fish and Wildlife Service in Alaska, Revised Region 7, memorandum QIPC, *Bear Safety Policies,* August 2, 1995, 7; Department of Renewable Resources, Government of the Northwest Territories, *Safety in Bear Country,* rev. ed. (Yellowknife, 1992).

42. John Stevens, Wrangell Ranger District, Tongass National Forest, phone conversation with author, October 1996.

43. Ontario Ministry of Natural Resources, *Wilderness Guide to Quetico Provincial Park,* brochure QS-R140-000-BB1 (published by authority of The Minister of the Environment Minister of Supply and Services Canada, 1990).

44. Stephen Herrero and Andrew Higgins, "Field Use of Capsaicin Sprays as a Bear Deterrent," in *Proceedings, 10th International Conference on Bear Research and Management* (Fairbanks: IUCN Bear Specialists Group, 1995).

45. Craig Medred, "Pepper Spray? Bad Bet," *Anchorage Daily News,* October 6, 1996.

46. One example is by Gary Turbak, "A Defensive Solution: When Bear Meets Man, a Spray Derived from Red Peppers May Save the Day," *Field & Stream,* June 1987, 59, 109–10.

47. For a summary of the situation, see Tom Kenworthy, "Wrestling with a Bear of a Problem in the Western Wilderness," *Washington Post,* November 21, 1994, and Mark L. Shaffer, *Keeping the Grizzly Bear in the American West: A Strategy for Real Recovery,* The Wilderness Society, October 8, 1992, 17 pp.

48. Ben Long, "Forest Timber Goes $2.8 Million in Red," *Kalispell (Montana) Daily Inter Lake,* March 15, 1995.

49. Michael Garrity, "Conservation Biology Alternative for Grizzly Bear Population Restoration in the Greater Salmon–Selway Region of Central Idaho and Western Montana," *Alliance for the Wild Rockies, Special Report,* no. 8, January 1980.

50. Scott Sonner, "Democrats Target Mine, Timber, Grazing Subsidies," *Anchorage Daily News,* January 28, 1995.

51. John Weiss, "Yellowstone Grizzly Hunts Foreseen," *Outdoor Life,* March 1980.

52. For the first study, see K. Aune and W. Kasworn, *East Front Grizzly Bear Study; Final Report* (Helena: Montana Department of Fish, Wildlife, and Parks, 1989), and for the second, U.S. Department of the Interior, National Park Service, Interagency Grizzly Bear Study Team, *Effects of Access on Human-Caused Mortality of Yellowstone Grizzly Bears,* by D. J. Mattson and R. R. Knight, Rept. 1991 (Bozeman, Mont., 1991).

53. Adolph Murie, "Cattle on Grizzly Bear Range," *Journal of Wildlife Management* 12 (1948): 57–72.

54. "Conflict between Grizzlies and Cows Takes New Twist," *Yellowstone Grizzly Journal* 8, no. 3 (Fall 1995): 7.

55. B.C. Ministry of Environment, Lands and Parks, *Conservation of Grizzly Bears in British Columbia,* Background Rept., 1995, 70 pp.

56. Douglas H. Chadwick, "Grizz: Of Men and the Great Bear," *National Geographic,* February 1986, 213.

recommended references

BOOKS

Beecham, John J., and Jeff Rohlman. *A Shadow in the Forest: Idaho's Black Bear.* Boise: Idaho Department of Fish and Game; Moscow: University of Idaho Press, 1994. Although the writing is a bit dry and academic, the facts are exciting. This is essential reading for conservationists.

Fair, Jeff. *The Great American Bear.* Minoqua, Wis.: NorthWord Press, 1990. Covers basic black bear biology as well as bear conservation efforts and bear–human interactions. It's accurate and easy to read.

Lynch, Wayne. *Bears: Monarchs of the Northern Wilderness.* Seattle, Wash.: Mountaineers Books, 1993. If you want just one book that gives in-depth coverage about the biology and ecology of black bears, grizzly bears, and polar bears, this is it.

Peacock, Doug. *Grizzly Year.* New York: Henry Holt and Company, 1990. Native Americans called grizzlies the "medicine bear." This is a real-life story of how the medicine bear heals the spiritual wounds of a Vietnam vet. Bear biology, wilderness philosophy, and wonderful writing.

Rogers, Lynn. *Watchable Wildlife: The Black Bear.* 1992. North Central Distribution Center, One Gifford Pinchot Drive, Madison, WI 53705-2398. This U.S. Forest Service brochure provides a great capsule summary (eighteen pages) about black bears and how to get along with them.

Shepard, Paul, and Barry Sanders. *The Sacred Paw: The Bear in Nature, Myth, and Literature.* New York: Viking Penguin, 1985. Even if the closest you've ever been to a bear is eating a bear claw pastry from a bakery, this book shows how deeply bears are ingrained in our conscious and subconscious minds.

Walker, Tom. *River of Bears.* Stillwater, Minn.: Voyageur Press, 1993. A special book about a special place—Alaska's McNeil River—that offers an enlightened view of bears.

VIDEOS

On the Trail of Pennsylvania's Black Bears. Pennsylvania Game Commission, 2001 Elmerten Avenue, Harrisburg, PA 17110-9797; (717) 787-7015. Provides comprehensive coverage about the behavior, biology, and habits of black bears.

Way of the [Brown] Bear in Alaska. Distributed by Bullfrog Films, P.O. Box 149, Oley, PA 19547; 1-800-543-3764, http://www.bullfrogfilms.com. Focuses entirely on bear behavior.

index

aggression, defensive vs. predatory 17
Aumiller, Larry 74, 80
avoidance: bear-bear 20–22, 60, 64, 70, 74; bear-human 60, 64, 70–71, 74, 99

bear bells 61, 65–66
bear behavior 9, 15–23, 74, 85–86
bear management 99
bear resistant food containers 47–48, 51, 54
bears, physical description and senses 24–27
beer 51
binoculars 46, 63
bluff charges 82–83
boaters 18–19, 44, 47, 53, 59, 76; campsite selection 57; rest stops 63–64, 69
body language 9, 17, 22–23, 79–86

campsite selection 56–57, 64
carcasses/carrion 64
charges 22, 58, 60 *illus.*, 71, 73, 78, 82–84, 87
children, and bears 13–14; and pepper spray 89–90
confrontations/encounters 15, 20–23, 43, 56, 59–60, 64, 79–86, 91
cooking 43–45

cross-country skiing 23, 68, 77–78. *See also* winter travel.
cubs, defense of 15–16, 58, 84
curiosity 17–19

day beds 65
dogs 58–59
dominance and subordination between bears 9, 22–23

encounters/confrontations 15, 20–23, 43, 56, 59–60, 64, 79–86, 91

Endangered Species Act 93–101
ethical issues 61–62, 72–75, 76–78
evolutionary differences, black vs. brown bear 15–16
eye contact 80

fight or flight response 15–16
fishing 75–76
food: bear diet 28, 41, 68; conditioning of bears 18, 20, 41–42, 59; seasonal use by bears 11, 28, 68; storage by humans 41–55
French, Steve 27, 64, 67, 80, 86, 92

garbage 41–42, 48, 52–53
Grizzly Bear Recovery Plan 93–101
group size 8, 66–67, 86
growling 22

guns 87–88
habituation 20, 68
hearing 27
Herrero, Stephen 7, 37, 73
Hessing, Polly 16, 79
hibernation 27
home ranges 16
hunting 71, 95

injuries, minimizing 85–86
intelligence 8, 17–18

Jonkel, Chuck 88–89

livestock: conflicts with bears 70, 93–101; taxpayer costs 94
logging and logging roads 93–101

"magic circle" 16, 59, 70, 72
Manning, Harvey 76–77
menstruation 8, 29–39; advice for women 38–39
mountain biking 76–78
Muir, John 41

noise, alerting bears with 8, 61–67, 69, 77, 81
North Cascades 97–99

Peacock, Doug 18, 66–67
pepper spray 80, 88–92
personal space 16. See also "magic circle."
petroleum products 18–19, 53
photography 9, 59, 66–67, 72–75

planning, pre-trip 11–14
playing dead 79–80, 83–86
predation, on humans: 17, 57, 80–82; on wildlife 17
research 99–100
Rogers, Lynn L. 37, 58
running from bears 7, 26, 79, 82

salivation 21–22, 80
Selway-Bitterroot 100–101
sexual activity (human) 39–40
speed of bears 26
Stonorov, Derek 22, 39–40
subordination and dominance between bears 9, 22–23
swimming 59

tents: 44; value as bear deterrent 57
territoriality 8–9, 15–16
trails 51, 57, 68–70
tree-climbing 7, 26, 75, 79, 82–83

unpredictable nature of bears 18, 20; of humans 72

vision 26–27, 61

whistling 65
winter travel 23, 27, 68. See also cross-country skiing
women, menstruating 8, 29–39; advice for 38–39. See also menstruation

yawning 8, 12 illus., 15, 22

ABOUT THE AUTHOR

Dave Smith is a naturalist who has lived in grizzly country since 1972. He has worked in Yellowstone, Glacier, Glacier Bay, and Denali National Parks, and worked as a fire lookout in northwest Montana for three summers. Dave's outdoor adventures have included a solo canoe trip from Yellowstone National Park to the Missouri River in North Dakota and a forty-day stay in the remote, rarely visited desert canyons in central Arizona.

Dave lectures widely on bears and has appeared with Jack Hanna in a documentary on Glacier Bay National Park aired by PBS and The Nature Channel. He is the author of *Alaska's Mammals,* and resides in Anchorage, Alaska.

Other titles you may enjoy from The Mountaineers:

ANIMAL TRACKS Books and Posters, *Chris Stall*
Tracks and information on 40-50 animals common to each region.
Volumes for: Alaska, California, Northern California, Southern California, Great Lakes, Mid-Atlantic, New England, Pacific Northwest, Rocky Mountains, Southeast, Southwest, and Texas.

BEARS: Monarchs of the Northern Wilderness, *Wayne Lynch*
Large format, full-color book explores bears' life cycles, communication, habits, relationships, and daily life.

PREGNANT BEARS AND CRAWDAD EYES: Excursions & Encounters in Animal Worlds, *Paul Schullery*
Twenty-one essays illuminate the practical life of animals and how they are affected and perceived by humans.

WILDERNESS BASICS, 2nd Ed.: The Complete Handbook for Hikers & Backpackers, *Jerry Schad & David S. Moser, editors*
Comprehensive resource covers all aspects of backcountry use: planning, equipment, navigation, weather; coastal, mountain, and desert travel; first aid, and winter mountaineering.

STAYING FOUND, 2nd Ed.: The Complete Map and Compass Handbook, *June Fleming*
Updated and revised handbook presents easy-to-use, unified map-and-compass system. Includes instruction on route planning, winter navigation, teaching kids to "stay found," coping when you're lost, and more.

MOUNTAINEERING FIRST AID, 4th Ed.: A Guide to Accident Response and First Aid Care, *Jan D. Carline, Steven C. MacDonald, Martha J. Lentz*
A team of medical experts provides expert, straightforward first aid instruction for outdoor enthusiasts. Conforms to the latest MOFA classes.

MEDICINE FOR MOUNTAINEERING & OTHER WILDERNESS ACTIVITIES, 4th Ed., *James A. Wilkerson, M.D., editor*
Thoroughly revised and updated "bible" written by climber/physicians for travelers more than 24 hours away from medical aid, and for climbing expeditions.

THE MOUNTAINEERS, founded in 1906, is a nonprofit outdoor activity and conservation club, whose mission is "to explore, study, preserve, and enjoy the natural beauty of the outdoors. . . . " Based in Seattle, Washington, the club is now the third-largest such organization in the United States, with 15,000 members and five branches throughout Washington State.

The Mountaineers sponsors both classes and year-round outdoor activities in the Pacific Northwest, which include hiking, mountain climbing, ski-touring, snowshoeing, bicycling, camping, kayaking and canoeing, nature study, sailing, and adventure travel. The club's conservation division supports environmental causes through educational activities, sponsoring legislation, and presenting informational programs. All club activities are led by skilled, experienced volunteers, who are dedicated to promoting safe and responsible enjoyment and preservation of the outdoors.

If you would like to participate in these organized outdoor activities or the club's programs, consider a membership in The Mountaineers. For information and an application, write or call The Mountaineers, Club Headquarters, 300 Third Avenue West, Seattle, WA 98119; (206) 284-6310.

The Mountaineers Books, an active, nonprofit publishing program of the club, produces guidebooks, instructional texts, historical works, natural history guides, and works on environmental conservation. All books produced by The Mountaineers are aimed at fulfilling the club's mission.

Send or call for our catalog of more than 300 outdoor titles:

The Mountaineers Books
1001 SW Klickitat Way, Suite 201
Seattle, WA 98134
1-800-553-4453 / e-mail: mbooks@mountaineers.org